The Child Abuse–Delinquency Connection

The Child Abuse–
Delinquency Connection

David N. Sandberg
Boston University

Lexington Books
D. C. Heath and Company/Lexington, Massachusetts/Toronto

Library of Congress Cataloging-in-Publication Data

Sandberg, David N.
  The child abuse-delinquency connection.

  1. Juvenile delinquency—United States.   2. Child
abuse—United States.   I. Title.
HV9104.S3153   1989   362.7'044   87-45844
ISBN 0-669-17022-4 (alk. paper)

REV.

Published simultaneously in Canada
Printed in the United States of America
International Standard Book Number: 0-669-17022-4
Library of Congress Catalog Card Number 87-45844

The paper used in this publication meets the minimum requirements of American National
Standard for Information Sciences—Permanence of Paper for Printed Library Materials,
ANSI Z39.48-1984. ∞™

89 90 91 92 8 7 6 5 4 3 2 1

To my mother, Janice, the memory of my father, Lars, my brother, Peter, and his wife, Nancy.

In spite of all that has been said and written on the subject of juvenile delinquency, there is little understanding of the problems of the children who are called juvenile delinquents. Lurid headlines and sensational newspaper accounts play up the superficial aspects of the subject, while the real story of what goes on in the hearts and minds of youthful offenders remains untold.

Perhaps these are other people's children, not yours or mine, or even our neighbors'. But the time has passed when we can ignore their troubles. Just as we now know that smallpox in the slums constitutes a danger to the homes in our garden districts, so do we know that human failure, whether it be in high places or hovels, affects us, our families, our communities, and ultimately the nation.

—Hon. A.V. Levy (Juvenile Court Judge)
Other People's Children (1956)

A stable, loving homelife is essential to a child's physical, emotional, and spiritual well-being. It requires no citation of authority to assert that children who are abused in their youth generally face extraordinary problems developing into responsible, productive citizens.

—Chief Justice William Rehnquist
United States Supreme Court
Santosky v. Kramer, 455 U.S. 790 (1982)

Contents

Foreword

Hon. Betty D. Friedlander

As one of my more demanding law school professors often said, the difficulty is not so much in finding the right answers, but in asking the right questions. In this collection of interviews with people who represent all aspects of juvenile justice, David Sandberg is posing in various forms fundamental questions challenging some of the underlying premises of our juvenile justice system.

If, as the people interviewed by Sandberg unanimously conclude, disproportionately large numbers of delinquents processed in the juvenile courts have themselves been victims of maltreatment and bear its traumatic consequences, do we not have to question whether or not maltreatment predisposes children to later incorrigibility, delinquency, or other antisocial behavior? If there is a predisposing effect, should we not explore with much more vigor than we have to date whether programs for the prevention and remediation of child abuse and neglect may also be effective in preventing and reducing delinquency?

In view of the complexity of maltreatment and its profound influence on the child's emotional, psychological, and behavioral capacities, do we need to reconsider the adequacy of our present theories about how to treat the young people already in the system, in order to reduce their delinquent or antisocial behavior?

If significant numbers of delinquents have been victims of maltreatment, what are the implications for the current movement toward an even more punitive juvenile justice model that espouses primary goals of personal accountability and punishment in accord with "just deserts?"

We already know a good deal about some of these issues. Research such as Alfaro's major study of abused, neglected, and delinquent children in New York and their families, a study discussed in this book, and many other studies, confirm overwhelmingly that maltreatment in childhood is significantly associated with delinquency. In addition, the evidence suggests the more severe and long-lasting the maltreatment, the more violent the criminal behavior.

An extensive body of studies in the field of child abuse and neglect documents the severe physical, psychological, and neurological consequences of maltreatment, and the various ways in which they may impair the child's capacity to integrate socially. Within the last ten years, a growing body of interdisciplinary studies has been establishing strong associations between inadequate parental nurture, harsh or erratic discipline, and delinquent and violent behavior in later childhood and adolescence. Related studies show that parental education programs emphasizing nonphysical disciplinary techniques improve the parent-child relationship and may be effective in reducing delinquency and other antisocial behavior.

This research, taken together with the observations of professionals who work in the field of juvenile justice, such as those who have been interviewed for this book, strongly suggests the need for a broadly based reconceptualization of the fields of delinquency, child protection, and child welfare, so as to create a new, enlarged, interdisciplinary environment that will promote the development of juvenile crime-prevention strategies based on the prevention and remediation of child maltreatment.

It is not only that such new strategies may make more effective use of the limited resources available to control juvenile crime—a matter of great concern in a society where massive expenditures for penal institutions cannot keep pace with the increasing criminal population. More important, the development of maltreatment-preventive approaches to delinquency may be a matter of fundamental social fairness. For there is a fundamental injustice in assessing full responsibility and imposing sanctions for juvenile misconduct or crimes committed by young people whose very capacity to conform their behavior to societal standards has been impaired by abuse or chronic neglect experienced at vulnerable developmental periods in their lives. While society has been protective of the procedural rights of young people processed in the juvenile justice system ever since the 1967 Supreme Court decision in *Gault,* it has not yet questioned whether substantial justice and fundamental fairness require a recognition of the incapacitating effects of childhood maltreatment and a special solicitude for those juvenile offenders whose mental and behavioral capacities have been damaged.

As Sandberg and the professionals in this book stress, society clearly needs, for safety as well as coherence, to focus on juvenile misbehavior in proportion to the gravity of the criminal act in order to discourage future violations, and to impose restrictive measures when necessary to prevent harm to others. But the punitive element in juvenile justice sanctions—inherently expressive of society's condemnation—raises some deeply troubling questions of fairness when applied to adolescent offenders who are also the victims of serious physical, sexual, and emotional abuse or neglect.

The challenge to create within the juvenile justice system concurrent approaches to crime prevention and treatment based on principles of child and adolescent development is repeatedly issued, implicitly and explicitly, within the interviews that form the core of this book. These personal and professional observations of experienced people in the system reinforce what research and prevention efforts are beginning to demonstrate—that maltreated children face special obstacles in assuming responsibility for their behavior, they may not respond well to traditional methods of treatment, and they do not benefit from punitive sanctions.

If the juvenile justice system is ever going to fulfill a role in preventing delinquency and reducing recidivism, it is essential that this message be conveyed beyond the community of professionals and that it be understood by the public, which ultimately shapes public policy. David Sandberg, through these interviews and his other works on maltreated adolescents, is building a professional and public agenda to explore the merger of new and existing juvenile justice initiatives premised on the relationship between juvenile crime and child maltreatment.

Based on our present knowledge of how to prevent delinquency and reduce recidivism, this focus on the parent-child relationship as the context for prevention initiatives may present the most promising prospects for achieving real improvement in the effectiveness of juvenile justice, and at the same time provide a greater measure of social fairness to children at risk for antisocial, criminal, or violent behavior.

Acknowledgments

This book would not have been possible without the continuing support of the Boston University School of Law. I also want to recognize the National Center on Child Abuse and Neglect (NCCAN) for providing grant support in 1982–83 for a related project.

More than anything, this book has its roots in work done long ago when I was director of Odyssey House Inc. in Hampton, New Hampshire. It was at Odyssey House that I first heard delinquents disclose abuse histories.

In the early 1970s, there was little awareness of child abuse, and I was fortunate to be in the professional company of people such as Rowen Hochstedler, Pam Hagan, Bernard Litvin, Calvin Legg, and especially Judianne Densen-Gerber. We learned together, and I am pleased to acknowledge their contributions to my understanding of the abuse-delinquency connection.

Equally valuable were contributions by abused delinquents undergoing treatment at Odyssey House. They had the courage to speak, to tell the rest of us what had happened.

Lastly, my appreciation to José Alfaro, Jim Garbarino, Pam Hagan, Rowen Hochstedler, Judge William Jones, Patricia Shannon, Andrew Vachss, and Sterling Winslow for helping to tell the child abuse–delinquency story.

Definitions

W ithin the context of this book, *child abuse* is used broadly to include physical, sexual, and psychological abuse as well as neglect to avoid the cumbersome and repeated use of *child abuse and neglect*. The severity of the abuse that we talk about is sufficient to result in a finding of maltreatment as administratively or judicially determined under state child protection statutes. Editorial omission of the term *neglect* should not be construed as an indication that its effects are less harmful than the effect of physical, sexual, or psychological abuse. In fact, they are more harmful in many cases.

As is now widely known, *perpetrators of child abuse* include an array of adults, including parents, relatives, family friends, trusted community members, and strangers. Less well-known perpetrators include adolescents and preadolescents who are frequently themselves the victims of maltreatment. There is also child abuse perpetration, which comes under the heading of institutional abuse. However, this book is foremost concerned with the aforementioned perpetrators and parents in particular.

Concerning *delinquency,* nearly everyone agrees that the term includes those acts that if committed by an adult would be a misdemeanor or felony. Nearly all states have certification procedures whereby especially dangerous offenders (e.g., those charged with murder, attempted murder, and rape) may be tried as adults and forfeit juvenile justice protections accorded delinquents. Thus, *delinquency* does not encompass most of these offenders, at least within the context of this book.

Differences arise over whether the term should extend to status offenders (CHINS, PINS) who have truanted, run away, or become unmanageable but who have committed no crime. Many states distinguish the two to protect status offenders from incarceration—and justifiably so. However, from a mental health perspective, CHINS and delinquents are often indistinguishable, with similar histories of maltreatment. For this reason and because most CHINS have also committed delinquent acts, however minor and frequently undetected by authorities, *delinquency* is used here to include criminal and status offenses. We are also talking, principally, about recidivist delinquents.

Two other definitional issues are deserving of attention at the outset. First, this book mainly discusses the child abuse–delinquency connection in terms of preadolescent victims who eventually become delinquent in adolescence. In no way is this intended to suggest that children cease to be vulnerable to abuse once they become adolescents. For example, James and Anne Garbarino reported in 1982 that adolescents between the ages of eleven and seventeen constitute anywhere between one-fourth and one-third of all victims although it is not known for what percentage of these the abuse is a continuation or resumption from the preadolescent period.

Second, the abused and delinquent youth discussed in this book are those who come to the attention of administrative agencies and the courts. A well-known corollary of this is that a very high percentage of these youths come from lower socioeconomic families. Far less is known about abused and delinquent youth from upper socioeconomic families who often are able to avoid state intervention.

1
Opening Statement

David N. Sandberg

The origins of commentary on the relationship between child abuse and delinquency are unknown. Judge Bill Jones of Charlotte, North Carolina, often begins his presentations on the relationship by reading passages from *The Adventures of Huckleberry Finn*, especially the parts about Pap beating Huck and Huck then running away. Maybe Mark Twain was the first to be aware of the connection, and maybe Judge Jones is correct that Huck was the first abused delinquent to come to the public's attention.

My own introduction to the child abuse–delinquency connection, as forenoted, was in the early 1970s when I was director of a residential treatment program for court-referred delinquents. These young people were sent to us for theft, assault, breaking and entering, running away, being truant, using drugs—for just about everything except child abuse, which we later learned many had experienced. At that time, child abuse was just beginning to surface as a national issue and most professionals knew little more about it than the average citizen.

Prior to leading group therapy sessions for these young people, I had never heard of such brutal beatings, sexual assaults, verbal put-downs, neglect, and parental abandonment. Rather than coming forth openly, the residents told their life stories reluctantly and in fragments. The horror stories were bad enough, but hardest of all was hearing the residents defend the parents who had been brutal toward them since they were preschoolers. Only after some time did we come to realize that to condemn one's parents is to orphan one's self. This was their central dilemma.

Nevertheless, it took several years to get my anger at abusive parents under control so that I could begin to sort out how to counsel these child outcasts. Some staff never got this far and burned out. Others learned that their great anger at abusive parents often bore little or no resemblance to what many of these young victims were feeling about their parents.

Ironically, none of the people I worked with at that time ever gave much thought to a formal relationship between child abuse and delinquency. Like most others in the social service field, we were too busy trying to survive financially and emotionally. Plus, if no one else was talking about a relationship between child abuse and delinquency—and no one was, as far as we knew—there was no external confirmation that we had stumbled across something important.

It wasn't until 1982 when I returned to academia as a staff attorney that I began to realize some of the larger implications of the relationship. As part of my job at Boston University School of Law's Center for Law and Health Sciences, I daily reviewed the *Federal Register*. One day I noticed that the National Center on Child Abuse and Neglect (NCCAN) in Washington, D.C., was looking for someone to "examine" the relationship between child abuse and delinquency. At first, I scanned by the announcement. On a second glance, I saw my years of prior work with delinquents.

This was the first time I had ever seen or heard someone outside my own organization suggest that the relationship between child abuse and delinquency had special implications. I still was not clear about these implications, but, I was prepared to conduct a research inquiry and was awarded a grant from the National Center.

The project, entitled "The Role of Child Abuse in Delinquency and Juvenile Court Decision-making," was conducted in 1982–83 (see appendix A for selected findings). It is especially significant that the project began, rather than ended, with an assessment of the abuse rate for a sample delinquent population. Most prior research seemed to begin and end with prevalence rates, with little or no attempt made to explore other aspects of the relationship. One noteworthy exception was José Alfaro's 1970's study of delinquent and abused children in New York. It remains the best of the studies.

In addition to an initial determination of the prevalence of abuse among 150 delinquents, we asked the psychiatric members of the team to probe further into the abuse-delinquency connection. Although nonempirical and highly subjective, I am satisfied that it produced some of the more important statements in existence about how abuse-delinquency interrelate. Some of this analysis can be found in chapter 4.

In addition to producing four sets of research findings, the NCCAN project stimulated my interest in learning more about the child abuse–delinquency relationship as a body of knowledge. Was the child abuse component of many delinquents' lives as dramatic a factor as I thought it was? Was I over-emphasizing the abuse factor? Were many judges, probation officers, and practitioners in the field as unaware of the connection as they seemed to be? What practice or policy conclusions had emerged, if any? What body of knowledge and community of professionals did the abuse-delinquency relationship belong to? Was it primarily a delinquency or a child abuse phenomenon? Or did it belong in some new hybrid category? Most important, was the abuse-delinquency connection a major issue or was it a passing curiosity, an insignificant stepchild of delinquency or child abuse?

I am convinced that the child abuse–delinquency relationship is a major issue featuring a unique convergence of child abuse and delinquency elements. By this I mean that the connection encompasses more than just many delinquents have been abused when they were younger. For example, a teenage prostitute who was sexually abused in the home during preadolescence presents three basic phenomenon: He or she is an abuse victim and a delinquent, and something about the earlier sexual abuse seems to play an important part in the later prostitution. Another example is a teenager who commits acts of extreme violence and has a history of severe physical abuse as a young child. Again, three phenomenon are present: He or she is an abuse victim, and a delinquent, and something about the earlier, severe physical abuse very likely plays an important part in the later perpetration of violence.

The connection is undeniable, particularly in light of research that suggests that teenage prostitutes have unusually high rates of sexual abuse histories, just as very violent delinquents have unusually high rates of early physical abuse. Something is occurring within the third category that is critical to a better understanding of many delinquents.

There is other evidence in support of my contention that the child abuse–delinquency relationship is a major issue involving a unique interplay between these two phenomenon. It has a distinct history, perhaps beginning in earnest with the New York State Assembly Select Committee on Child Abuse, which solicited testimony during the early 1970s as a prelude to passing legislation. As José Alfaro observes,

> In preparing these legislative changes, the Select Committee held several series of hearings throughout the state over a three year period. This testimony emphasized that many professionals had observed that abused and neglected children often grow up to become problem children who returned to the care and attention of societal institutions as delinquent and ungovernable juveniles. Several family Court judges of long experience were especially emphatic about this. (from *Exploring the Relationship between Child Abuse and Delinquency*, Robert J. Hunner and Yvonne Elder Walker, eds. Montclair, N.J.: Allanheld, Osmun, 1981, p. 176.).

Were these hearings the first formal consideration of the abuse-delinquency relationship? There is no way of knowing. However, until someone can point to some earlier deliberation, they can be considered the starting point for societal inquiry into overlaps between child abuse and delinquency, something that stirred in the 1970s and blossomed in the 1980s.

The next significant event took place beyond the U.S. borders in Canada in 1975. The Canadian Senate was deliberating capital punishment, and some senators were troubled by their lack of knowledge about the causes of violent criminal behavior. Eventually, a Senate Subcommittee on Childhood Experiences as Causes of Criminal Behavior was formed. During 1977–78, the Subcommittee heard testimony from twenty-seven expert witnesses, received numerous briefs, and reviewed all relevant literature ranging from hyperkinesis to learning disabilities to alcoholism to child abuse. The subcommittee ultimately concluded that child abuse is one critical factor in the formation of criminal behavior, and violent behavior in particular. Thus, rather than placing child abuse at the center of things, the Subcommittee chose to view abuse as critical in the formation of later criminality when it coexists with several other factors such as parental alcoholism, being born to criminal parents, and/or growing up in a disintegrated family.

During the same general time period as the Canadian Senate was conducting its inquiry, a stateside conference was held in Seattle, Washington. This was the first multidisciplinary gathering in the United States to examine the child abuse–delinquency relationship. In retrospect, most of the conference presentations seem elementary. But these conferees were pioneers, among the first people to be asked to comment on the vexing relationship between child abuse and delinquency.

Another milestone was commencement of the forementioned 1982 National Center on Child Abuse and Neglect (NCCAN) research. The following year, the Senate Subcommittee on Juvenile Justice conducted a hearing on the "Relationship between Child Abuse, Juvenile Delinquency, and Adult Criminality" (see appendix B). Like many other governmental hearings, this one soon faded from memory. For one day, however, the United States Senate considered the relationship between child abuse and delinquency worthy of its consideration.

Another major event in 1983 was the National Conference of State Legislatures in Denver identifying the abuse-delinquency relationship as important enough to warrant briefing of the nation's state legislators. Actually, two briefings were held. One was in Washington, D.C., and the other in Boston. At least one legislature, Wyoming's, subsequently amended its delinquency statute to include the following provisions:

(a) After a [delinquency] petition is filed, the court shall order a probation officer, the county department of public assistance and social services or other qualified person or agency designated by the court to make a predisposition study and report covering:

  (i) The social history, environment and present condition of the child and his family;

  (ii) The performance of the child in school;

  (iii) *The presence of child abuse and neglect histories,* [emphasis added], learning disabilities, physical impairments and past acts of violence; and

  (iv) Other matter relevant to the child's present status as a delinquent, treatment of the child or proper disposition of the case.

Section (a)(iii) is taken directly from our chief recommendation in the 1982–83 NCCAN project—namely, that every delinquency code in the country should be amended to more sharply focus the predisposition study on state-of-the-art factors strongly associated with delinquency. Of foremost importance is requiring judicial inquiry about a youth's history of child abuse and neglect. The reasons for this are commented on at length in the chapters that follow.

The following year (1984), a multidisciplinary meeting was convened in Racine, Wisconsin. The group included researchers, practitioners, and policy makers, all with considerable expertise in child abuse and/or delinquency. Perhaps as significant as the conferees' findings and recommendations (see appendix C) was the coming together of such diverse individuals to examine the relationship. Equally significant was the involvement of three national organizations in bringing about the conference: the Office of Juvenile Justice and Delinquency Prevention and the National Center on Child Abuse and Neglect—and the National Committee for the Prevention of Child Abuse in Chicago, perhaps the largest and most influential private organization concerned with society's response to child maltreatment.

Despite this activity there has been a certain waning of interest since 1984, at least within academic and government circles. It may be that inertia has set in, notwithstanding a general consensus among academics and direct service workers that the relationship between child abuse and delinquency is an extremely important issue. We seem to be stuck at the point of not knowing where to go now that it has been established that delinquents have unusually high rates of maltreatment histories. One problem seems to be that sustained focus on just the child abuse factor is suggestive, at least in some people's minds, of a lack of sophistication. Researchers, in particular, tend to be wary of any unitheory explanation for complex human behavior. Certainly no one factor can explain delinquency or any other deviant conduct, but multifactor/multicause analyses have the unfortunate side-effect of discouraging a sustained effort to learn as much as we can about the role of child abuse in delinquency.

A related problem is that few professionals have "grown up" with the child abuse–delinquency relationship. It is a foreign subject to many, and one that has attracted academics only as a brief diversion from more mainstream pursuits within the child abuse or delinquency fields. Thus, for example, if one's academic work is in the child abuse field, overlaps with delinquency hold little lasting interest because abused delinquents comprise a small percentage of the nation's total abused population. Most researchers simply prefer studying populations that are more representative of the general population.

Delinquency researchers also have not pursued the child abuse factor more rigorously, which is less understandable, especially when renowned clinicians with a criminal justice bent such as Karl Menninger extoll the significance of the connection. Certainly, delinquency research receives less media attention and seemingly less funding than child abuse research, and less research is probably being done. It also appears that delinquency has been able to cross over into the child abuse research sector, however modestly, in a way that abuse has not been able to cross over into the delinquency sector.

But I have another explanation. I believe that the research community has provided the most important data—namely, that delinquents experience maltreatment at unusually high rates regardless of whether these youth are from New Hampshire, New York, Illinois, Arizona, or California.

The other vital research data we have in our possession is that the experience of child maltreatment is uniformly harmful, often very harmful. In fact, it would be difficult to identify any other childhood experience that has such well-documented destructive effects.

In short, the research community has spoken. But the data alone has not proven sufficient to inspire widespread new practice and policy based on the child abuse–delinquency relationship. Just as researchers tend to compartmentalize efforts, primarily within the child abuse or delinquency sector, so do direct service providers. Thus, in most states, different agencies are responsible for child abuse and delinquency. At the federal level, child abuse is under the jurisdiction of the Department of Health and Human Services whereas delinquency is under the jurisdiction of the Department of Justice. No doubt there are advantages to categorical organization, but promoting greater understanding of the interrelationship of foremost children and youth issues is not one of them.

How, then, are new practice and policy based on the child abuse–delinquency connection to come about?

I submit that the pathway to realizing these objectives lies with the continued testimony of individuals who have been involved with or affected by the relationship in special ways. Six of the eight people in the chapters that follow are on the frontlines of child abuse and delinquency. They have been for many years. The other two have greatly contributed to the emerging child abuse–delinquency field through their research and policy recommendations.

They are, by no means, the only people who are capable of telling the child abuse–delinquency story. In some respects, they resemble many people who through life experience or profession know how critical the child abuse–delinquency connection is. In other respects, principally through their long association with the connection and their having previously participated in formal assessments of child abuse, delinquency or the interrelationship of the two, they are unusual.

The story begins with Sterling Winslow.

2
A Victim's View

Sterling Winslow[a]

S terling Winslow was referred to Odyssey House New Hampshire at age sixteen by a juvenile court. He was the fourth of seven children. Neglected since birth, he also experienced physical abuse at the hands of alcoholic parents and from an older brother. He began to truant in the first grade and by age thirteen was using alcohol and drugs daily. He also regularly engaged in b&e's, theft, and violent destruction of property. He once used a pipe to smash twelve car windshields. Following treatment at Odyssey House, he attended a public high school, where he became a starting member of the football team and an honor roll student. Today, at twenty-seven, he is married, attends college, and has been a full-time counselor for delinquent youth for ten years.

Q: *What was your home situation like?*

A: I received a lot of physical abuse from my father. He'd use belts and wood paddles. My brothers and I would try to hide the paddles and sometimes they'd break when he hit us but he'd just make more. He took great pride in his paddles. With the belts, he'd usually hit us on the back, but sometimes he'd corner us in a room and just go berserk with the belt or paddle for fifteen minutes. He'd hit us anywhere. Once I got hit in the eye when he swung the buckle part of the belt. At other times, he hit me in the groin. He would also hit us with his fists. But usually it was the belts and the paddles. I had welts on my back from the beatings, and sometimes I was unable to go to school because they hurt so bad.

My mother was a very passive person who usually would come to me after a beating and say my father really didn't mean it, that he loved us. However, she also attacked me on a few occasions. Once, she threw a can of soup at me. It hit me in the head and I had to have seven stitches.

---

[a]Not his real name.

She was very worried afterwards and made me promise to tell the doctor that I accidentally hurt myself, which I did.

I also received a lot of abuse from a brother who was five years older than me. He constantly antagonized, teased, and beat me. Many of our fights were very violent, with me receiving most of the violence. Inevitably, he would blacken my eye, fatten a lip, or give me bruises. He was just always much bigger and won.

My older brother was also very psychologically abusive. He'd constantly tell me I was no good, I was stupid, I'd never amount to anything. He'd also tell my friends that I couldn't read and that I wet the bed, which I did until I was sixteen. He'd also set me up to get in trouble with my parents, and then take great pleasure when I got a beating. Because of his large size and exalted status in the family, I was totally captive to him, physically and mentally. It was a concentration camp type of thing that went on for years. I now know that my parents were also afraid of him.

He was also very abusive toward my other brothers and sisters. For example, he would lock my little brother in our basement, which had rats, and turn off the lights. My little brother was terrified. I knew I could not physically control my older brother, so if I was around I'd sneak into the basement to keep my little brother company. My older brother also delighted in torturing animals.

He really scared me. He was just very intense to live with—always tormenting and hurting me, and there was nothing I could do to escape from him. If he didn't beat or torment me, he'd break the few things I owned, and, being poor, I didn't own very much.

Q: *When did your father begin to physically abuse you?*

A: I was nine. It was about this time that my parents began to have serious marital problems. There was a lot of pressure in the household due to this. There was additional pressure due to there being seven kids by this time, my parents being poor, and my father's alcoholism.

Q: *Can you separate the abuse from the poverty you experienced or your parents' alcoholism, or does it all merge in the form of parents who had problems?*

A: I have learned positive things from being poor and never having had much. I know a lot of poor people who never abused their kids. But the abuse stands out as it is harder to accept than, say, parental alcoholism. Child abuse, in my opinion, is the worst thing you can do to someone. Even though I have been through a lot of therapy and done a lot with my professional life in the child abuse field, my own abuse is always with me. I still get tense when others are tense, and when people yell, I think back to my home. It's just that I now respond differently to the feelings. Instead of lashing out or using drugs, I talk with people. And I'm convinced that unless kids who have been abused get treatment, they are highly at risk to repeat the abuse.

Q: *How were you "disciplined" prior to age nine?*

A: With the hand, spankings. My father would make me drop my pants, put me over his knees, and hit me about ten times, then send me to my room where I would cry myself to sleep. He often would say when hitting me that this hurt him more, which I never understood.

Q: *What would set your father off? Did it require anything?*

A: It always involved my doing something "wrong," or someone telling him I had. One incident is vivid in my mind because it hurt me the most, psychologically. My parents were watching television one evening and I was in bed, supposedly asleep. I decided to go downstairs and tell them I loved them. When I got to the bottom of the stairs, I accidentally knocked over an open gallon of paint that had been left there. My dad just exploded and beat the shit out of me. He started punching me, picked me up, and threw me into a wall so hard my elbow actually went through the wall and into the adjoining bathroom. My mom freaked out. She was really scared, and for the rest of the night she tried to comfort me by saying he didn't mean it, that it was his drinking that made him do these things.

Q: *When you went to school with bruises, did anyone say or do anything?*

A: Some people noticed but they didn't do anything. In seventh grade, I told my guidance counselor what was going on at home. This was the first time I had ever told anyone. He told me it was wrong and that if it happened again I should call him at any time of day or night. Within days, my brother beat me badly again. My teeth went through my upper lip, I had two black eyes and an enormous scratch from my armpit to my waist. I called my guidance counselor and I wound up spending the night at his house. He, again, tried to reinforce that what was happening was not my fault. He also said if it ever happened again, he'd take pictures and we'd take legal action. Unfortunately, I got thrown out of school shortly thereafter and lost all contact with him.

Q: *When was this?*

A: Early 1970s. I was thirteen and in seventh grade. There was no child abuse reporting law at that time, or at least I don't think there was.

Q: *Was there any sexual abuse in your family?*

A: No. However, after my parents divorced one of my mother's boyfriends, also alcoholic, molested two of my younger sisters.

Q: *How old were you when the physical abuse stopped?*

A: My father's abuse stopped when I was thirteen, when my parents were divorced and my father left the house. However, with my father gone, my older brother's abuse became more intense. He became totally uncontrollable. He would also persuade my mother that I was really messing up and get her so worked up that she would take her fury out on me. I remember one night I came home and my brother told my mother that I had been smoking dope. He kept saying to her, "Look at his eyes! Look at his eyes!" My mother confronted me and then attacked me. She cornered me in the bathroom and clawed my face with her fingernails and pulled my hair. All the while, my brother stood behind my mother, smiling and gloating. I lost control. I punched the wall, ripped the phone off the wall, and left the house. The police came and talked to my mother and my brother. They persuaded the police that I was uncontrollable, a screwup, and an ingrate who made life hard for my mother.

When the police caught up with me, they told me what a creep I was for hitting my mother, which I hadn't done. They really did a number on me and had no interest in hearing my side of things. That incident was instrumental in turning me against the police. It was also the culmination of many police visits to our house. They had come on the average of once a week to break up fights between my older brother and me. In all those fights, I obviously had no chance of winning and was being seriously assaulted. Yet the police never took the time to find out what was going on. Also, my mother never called the police when my father beat me— only when my brother did. My subsequent delinquency, in part, was my attempt to get back at the police for that night and for all the previous times. They failed to protect me. Worse, they put me down as a jerk and a screwup, which only reinforced my feeling of being a bad person.

Q: *What were your feelings in those fights with your brother?*

A: I would go into a rage. I would get to the point where I didn't even feel the pain anymore. To understand, you have to imagine being pinned down in such a way that it is impossible to strike a blow or defend yourself, and you are being punched over and over again. You strain to get free, yet it does no good. The frustration and rage is so great that if you had a gun, you'd use it.

Q: *Did you ever reach a point when you really could have killed him?*

A: Yes. Once I stabbed him in the leg with scissors; another time, I threw a meat cleaver at his chest. It wasn't something I thought about. I was in a rage and I was just so tired of all the pain and torment. Even this worked against me, as he used these incidents to try to convince my mother that I was crazy, that I should be committed to a state hospital. This scared me because he was so powerful. I actually thought he could persuade her to do this and that I'd end up locked away for life. He was also very successful, as I said before, at persuading the police that I was the troublemaker. Then the police would reprimand me. He loved doing this.

Q: *Were you ever hospitalized?*

A: Just the one time I got the seven stitches when my mother threw the can of soup at me. I certainly could have been hospitalized on numerous other occasions. Once my brother fractured my collarbone. I've also injured my hand punching walls after being beaten up by my brother.

   Although not related to the violence, I twice had serious medical problems requiring hospitalization but my father wouldn't let my mother take me to the hospital. One turned out to be appendicitis. I hurt so badly I couldn't walk. I guess my father thought I was faking. He also said we couldn't afford a hospital bill. Finally, after three days, my mother had a cab take me to the hospital. The doctors opened me up just as my appendix ruptured. The other incident involved a scratch on my leg that became badly infected. Again, my parents said it wasn't serious and we couldn't afford a doctor. Finally, a neighbor who saw how inflamed my leg was told my parents, "Either you take him to the hospital or I will." My mother took me. It turned out I had blood poisoning, and I spent two weeks in the hospital. These two incidents really bothered me, as I was seriously ill and my parents did nothing to help me.

Q: *Did your parents verbally abuse you the way your brother did?*

A: No. My mother tried to be supportive, especially when I developed speech difficulties in elementary school. I had a hard time pronouncing words and, as late as fifth grade, I couldn't read or write. Some of my family members constantly threw this at me, especially my older brother who would call me "retarded" and "stupid." But my parents didn't do this type of thing.

Q: *And your parents never intervened?*

A: No. I could never understand why my mother never protected me. I later learned that she was afraid of my older brother. He hit her on numerous occasions. He also had many fist-fights with my dad. They'd yell at him to stop, although for some reason more often they yelled at me. I felt very vulnerable and unsafe in my own house. I hated my house. It was bad enough getting beaten but even worse to see one of my brothers being beaten and my being afraid to intervene. He even beat up my sisters.

Q: *How long did you have this feeling of fear and torment?*

A: From age nine until I was sixteen when things really escalated and I just began lashing out at anything and everybody. I just didn't care anymore.

Q: *It seems like what your older brother did to you goes beyond what we'd call "abuse" and, in fact, he tortured you? Is this accurate?*

A: The term "torture" fits for me because he laughed at and enjoyed what he was doing. Physical and psychological torture.

Q: *Did you experience mistreatment outside the home as well?*

A: Yes. For starters, I did not have a friend growing up. It was very lonely for me. I never had clean clothes, and I always smelled. We didn't have running water. My house was always filled with trash, including cat and dog feces. Consequently, all my peers put me down. I was the kid the others always giggled about, called "Stinky," and would never sit next to. I'd sneak into the lost-and-found to get a pair of mittens or a hat. Invariably, the kid who they belonged to would then accuse me of stealing them or hit me. I can remember always crying and even being afraid to go into the bathroom, where I'd usually get hit. There wasn't one person I felt safe with or who'd protect me. I was a real doormat. In later years, I began to fight back.

Q: *What about your teachers?*

A: I can remember a few who tried to be helpful, although none of them asked me about what was going on at home. When I was put in a special class in the fifth grade, which included what I now know were retarded children, I was convinced that I was stupid and no good. However, my speech therapist and another special education teacher eventually made me feel better about myself, at least for a while. I bonded to them, although we never talked about home. Once I got going, I excelled. There was no stopping me. You can't imagine how good it feels to be able to spell "dog," to be able to read a sentence. I did so well they had to mainstream me the next year. This was a big ego boost. Deep down, I always wanted to improve myself and not be a bully like my father and brother. Unfortunately, as soon as I entered junior high school, I started doing poorly again.

Q: *How poor was your family?*

A: Very poor. I was always hungry and never had proper clothing. Every year, my family would get a Christmas package from the local fire station. At holiday time, all the kids at school were asked to bring canned goods for needy people. Some kids would just give me a can or two and say, "Here, it's going to you, anyway." My family had a very bad reputation in town. I felt a lot of shame being a "Winslow." I'd cry myself to sleep wishing we could do fun things as a family.

Q: *How did all this make you feel?*

A: I really came to identify myself as a victim. All of these things were beyond my control. I could not help it that we were poor or that I was dirty or that my father and older brother assaulted me almost every day of my life. I began to search for answers and, of course, being a child, I did not blame my parents. At first, I blamed myself. Later, I began to blame the police because they were constantly at our house and never did anything to stop the violence. I wasn't able to trust others.

Nonetheless, in my preadolescent years I would periodically tap into feelings I had about never giving up, to keep trying. Batman, Robin, and Superman were my heroes because they overcame everything. Also, I would do things like shovel snow for elderly neighbors and not charge them. I got some good feelings from this.

Q: *Did you think that all other families were like yours?*

A: At first, yes. Being undereducated, I had no idea of the world beyond my home and school, which for me, were violent places. Also, a very disturbed family lived next to us and I was exposed to a lot of sick sexual stuff at a very early age—fathers in bed with their daughters, brothers bragging about "screwing their sisters."

Q: *When did you begin to realize that the treatment you were receiving at home was not normal?*

A: About age eight or nine. I didn't understand it, but I began to sense that other kids were not treated the way I was. Also, I knew a little more about the world from TV programs. The big awakening was when I told my guidance counselor what was going on at home, and he told me all that had happened to me was wrong, which I had long felt.

Q: *Once you firmly felt or realized the maltreatment was wrong, what did you do?*

A: I lashed out against everything, including myself. I wanted to die. I tried to commit suicide several times. I began to self-mutilate. I put cigarettes out on my arm, and carved tattoos on myself. I felt I was no good, a bad person, helpless, with no one to lean on. I really got in touch with hatred toward my parents, my brother, life—even wealthy people, whom I blamed for having so much. I started asking, "Why me?" I felt tremendous anger and self-pity. The burning desire to do well, which I had always had, began to fade. I was thirteen, and my attitude began to be, "If someone is going to give me shit, they're going to get shit back."

Q: *You said earlier it was also at thirteen that your father left the home. Did you feel relief at his departure?*

A: In some way, yes. On the other hand, no because his leaving meant that I would never have the father I had always fantasized about. He forced me to accept, at a very young age, that he would never be what I hoped he would. Also, and strangely enough, his presence in the home provided some measure of control over my older brother, who was totally abusive toward all of us once my father left.

Q: *Looking back at all the abuse, is there one message you got from it as a child, more than anything else?*

A: That I was not a good person, that I was stupid and ugly, and that I'd never amount to anything, and that, no matter how hard I'd try, it wouldn't do any good.

Q: *And how did this overall message affect your growing up?*

A: Well, I was enuretic until age sixteen; schooling was extremely difficult; I increasingly acted out; and ultimately, I just wanted to defy everybody. I just didn't care about myself; my primary goal was to "survive."

Q: *If you had not been abused or neglected and all the other family dynamics such as the alcoholism remained the same, do you think you would have become delinquent or as delinquent?*

A: The likelihood of my becoming delinquent would not have been as great. I likely would have "tested" like all adolescents, but I would not have done major acting out. Certainly, the intensity of my delinquency would have been much less.

It was the intensity of my father and brother's abuse, the physical pain and concentration camp—like atmosphere that eventually put calluses on my good feelings. And if I had acted out, it would not have been as aggressively. Most of my crimes were very aggressive, violent. They say a lot. I guess I expressed my anger and confusion through them.

Q: *What did your delinquency consist of?*

A: Many break-ins. The kids who were with me would go right into the bedrooms for the jewelry, but I would go for the refrigerator because I was always hungry. I'd also set aside some food and clothing to take home because my mother would not be as mad at me if I brought something home. Then I'd just go crazy, smashing everything in the house we broke into. I remember one day, it was my birthday and no one in my family even remembered it. My father had said he was coming over to the house to take me out. He never showed, which I knew deep down he wouldn't. I took a bunch of pills, drank some liquor, and then headed to a business establishment, which I just destroyed. I went berserk for two hours. Why no one heard or called the police, I'll never understand.

When I got through, I went down the street to a car lot. I saw a pipe on the ground and, without even thinking, I smashed a car windshield. A feeling of euphoria came over me and my adrenaline level was higher than it had ever been. I then just went down a long row of cars in the lot and smashed all the windshields. Twelve cars in all.

I also did a lot of other things, almost all involving violence.

Q: *Did you have any guilt over all the destruction and havoc you were responsible for as a delinquent?*

A: While I was committing a crime, no. As soon as I hit something with my fist and felt pain, I'd just become enraged. I'm sure the rage was also related to my being helplessly held on the ground all those years by my brother and just being pounded over and over. Immediately afterward, I would feel relieved and relaxed. But by the time I got home, I'd begin to feel badly. Sometimes, I'd even take something that I had stolen back to the house and leave it on the front doorstep or in the yard.

Q: *This suggests a close connection between your being repeatedly, physically assaulted as a child and your subsequent violent delinquency?*

A: There is no doubt about it. If you had asked me ten years ago, I'd have said the violence was due to my drinking. But I now know I was not born with all the rage I had. The intensity of the violence I expressed as an adolescent was equal to the intensity of my feelings of laying on the ground, being helplessly beaten and tormented, and just wanting to kill to make the assault stop.

Q: *Was your violence ever directed at people?*

A: Not unless I was attacked or threatened. I never wanted to hurt people through direct assault. I did on one occasion lose my temper and beat up my younger brother and sister and I felt very badly about this. I still feel badly. However, I do take some consolation in the fact that I was the only brother who gave to them, cared for them, and tried to protect them.

Q: *What were the other factors, if any, contributing to your delinquency?*

A: As I indicated previously, the police. All those years, they came to my house and never once took my side or protected me. Worse, they berated me for making things hard for my mother. The climactic event was a day when I was thirteen, and someone stole my ten-speed bike, which was the only present my father ever gave me. It meant everything to me. I went to the police station to report the theft and was asked the model number, bike manufacturer—questions I couldn't answer. They told me I shouldn't be making complaints unless I had this information. This was prior to my getting into delinquent activity. I walked away feeling totally humiliated. The experience just added to the growing feeling of no longer caring. I swore I'd get back at the police and never trust them.

Also, I know that part of my acting out was to get back at my father for all the things he did and didn't do, and at my mother for not protecting me. I also did it to embarrass my older brother, who was trying to look good in the community. There were other causative ingredients to my delinquency, including my inability to trust anyone and a growing feeling that the only way I'd ever get anything was to take it.

Peer acceptance was another factor. I hung out with a very negative group whose family experiences were similar to mine or so I thought at the time. Within our group, my nickname was "Wildman." I got this for doing things like playing chicken in front of speeding cars and crossing bridges hand-over-hand on the outer side of the walkway. Things like that, which involved risking my life. I received a lot of attention for this as well as my delinquency. Kids would talk about how cool I was. I got warm feelings from this even though I often felt terrible about my crimes, but I couldn't tell my peers that. Mind you, I did not fully realize these things at the time. It was only after a lot of painful therapy sessions.

Q: *If we could jump ahead just for a moment, what about today? How do you handle anger?*

A: I still get angry, even to the point of wanting to be very aggressive. But I have learned positive outlets—talking or aggressive sporting activity. While undergoing treatment at Odyssey House, I was eventually allowed to go to public high school, where I played football. Whenever I tackled a runner, I always had a mental picture of my father or brother.

Q: *Did your delinquent conduct cause abusive reactions by your parents or anyone else?*

A: What comes to mind is one cop who took great delight in harrassing me. Many times he threatened to "beat the hell" out of me. He'd also do things like drive by, give me the finger, and smile. There is no doubt, even now when I think about it, that he was way overstepping his boundaries and provoking me. He reminded me of home, especially of my brother— the abuse, the double messages, being two-faced, all creating the feeling that no one's going to help. And then everyone wondered why I retaliated against the police, doing things like ripping off the police station and demolishing a cruiser. That particular cop was as negative as I was. At the time, I generalized my feelings to include all cops. I've since come to appreciate that not all cops are like he was.

At home, my father was gone by the time I really began acting out. My mother was afraid to deal with me, which led to her relying more and more on my older brother. This set him up to become very abusive toward me.

Q: *Did any of your siblings not become delinquent and, if so, how do you account for this?*

A: All of my brothers and sisters, except for my youngest sister, became delinquent. Even today, she and I are the only ones who are doing well. The others, collectively, are welfare-dependent, lacking in motivation, involved with drugs and alcohol, entangled in destructive relationships, and/or carry a lot of anger. All of the abuse-related feelings that I expressed in therapy and playing football, they are still expressing in destructive ways.

My sister who made it dealt with all the family chaos by losing herself in education. School was her savior. She was also my mother's confidant and derived a lot of positive recognition through fulfilling this role. Today, she has a good job, is not angry, and has a good outlook on life. We're very close.

Q: *Your delinquency and maltreatment as a child were severe, yet you are well in control of your life. What accounts for this?*

A: When I started to really act out, I was placed in my aunt's home where for the first time in my life I experienced a family where there was no violence, where people cared about each other. I didn't fully appreciate their home, and I went on to get into more trouble. Ultimately, the court sent me to Odyssey House where, again, I had clean clothes, food, a decent room to sleep in, and no violence. Actually, I ran away after three days and was picked up by two state troopers, who beat the living hell out of me. I was in jail, as low as I'd ever been. Then I was told Odyssey House would take me back. Just getting another chance meant something. At Odyssey House, I was able to talk about all the negative tapes that constantly played through my mind: "You're no good, you'll never succeed." Eventually, these negative messages were replaced by a belief that I could be a good person, that I could succeed, that I had the ability and responsibility to create the type of life I wanted for myself.

As for where my desire to improve myself came from, I'm not sure. I do know I was always in touch with my emotional pain, which influenced me in not wanting to inflict pain on other people. Between ages thirteen and sixteen, I stopped caring and became very violent, although, fortunately, most of this was directed at property.

All of this is a constant reminder to me. One reason I think I am able to work well with young kids in trouble who come from chaotic families is that it doesn't take much for me to understand how helpless and frustrated they feel and why they lash out.

Q: *How central were the abuse and neglect to your therapy at Odyssey House?*

A: Very central. In order for me to make changes within myself, I had to deal with the abuse and the rage. These things affected everything I did and thought. I was cynical, explosive, and nontrusting. And it took a while for me to reveal the abuse to my therapist.

When I first came to Odyssey House, I was a behavior problem, which delayed more deep-rooted therapy. Also, I started out by telling the staff that everything was fine at home and my parents were great.

Q: *Why did you say this?*

A: I had a long history of getting hurt whenever I tried to let people in on what I was feeling. Also, I was afraid of what they would think of me if they knew what was really going on at home. It took me a long time to accept what the staff was telling me—namely, that it was okay to let out what I was really feeling.

When I finally did reveal some of my abuse, I was amazed to learn that others in my group had had similar experiences. This gave me a sense of unity, even family, which is something I never had before. Slowly, I learned that I was not going to be negatively judged for either my abuse or my own wrongdoing. I also saw some people with abuse histories as bad as mine who graduated from Odyssey House. All of this began to offer me hope that I, too, could make it.

Q: *How did you overcome your schooling deficits?*

A: When I came to Odyssey House at age sixteen, I read at a second-grade level and wrote at a third-grade level. And even though I received valuable help in the fifth grade from two special education teachers, I continued to feel dumb, perhaps even retarded.

Through counseling and Odyssey House's educational program, I came to understand that I was not dumb, that whereas other kids had peace of mind to study, I did not because of the constant hunger and being beaten. Once I got this in perspective, my confidence grew. With confidence, I was willing to take some risks, educationally speaking. Then one day, the Odyssey House teachers asked me if I wanted to go back to public school. I decided I would. I began to regain the desire to do well. I went on to be an honor roll student in public high school and eventually graduated. For me, a G.E.D. wasn't enough. I had to have a high school diploma.

Q: *What have you done, educationally, since graduating from high school?*

A: Since graduating from high school, I have worked full-time, and have attended college part-time. I'm working toward a B.S. degree in the human services field. I have forty credits and am hoping to receive up to two years' life-experience credit. After the B.S. degree, I plan to get right to work on an M.S.W. degree. My ultimate goal is to have my own counseling practice, specializing in family therapy. I also have interest in prevention work. The bottom line for me is that I no longer feel that anything is holding me back. I am a free person.

Q: *What if Odyssey House had not been attuned to maltreatment and, for example, adopted a "from this day forward" approach or simply concentrated on such things as your behavior or job training?*

A: The abuse would have continued to haunt me. I can see it in my family members today. My brothers, for example, are in their twenties and thirties, yet their hatred and anger is as intense as mine was in early adolescence. I was able to express most of my anger constructively, primarily through counseling sessions but also through such things as volunteering for all the most strenuous jobs at Odyssey House while I was a resident and slamming into blocking sleds when I played high school football. I processed my rage; my brothers never have. However, even today, I can get in touch with some pretty angry feelings. But I know where they come from and I know what to do about them.

Q: *Was it necessary for you to come to terms with your parents' maltreatment of you in order to get your life on a positive track, or is it something that one simply can't accept?*

A: I had to come to terms with my denial and, finally, acknowledge that regardless of all the pressures on my parents, what they did to me was wrong.

Q: *Having come to see that the home environment had been very harmful to you as a child, what responsibility, if any, did you feel for your younger siblings who were still at home?*

A: I felt a tremendous feeling of responsibility. After I had been in treatment for a while, I took my mother to court to have my younger sisters and brother removed from the home. This was an extremely hard thing for me to do and I was blacklisted by all the other family members. As it turned out, I was only partially successful. The investigating social workers kept saying that just because my family was poor did not mean it was an abusive family. In fact, there was not only physical abuse in my house but the kids were not eating properly. There was no hot water or heat. Some of my mother's boyfriends were bringing drugs into the house, and one of the boyfriends sexually assaulted my two sisters.

I felt terrible but, finally, some good things did happen. The state welfare people got my mother a furnace and did such things as replace all the windows and increase my mother's food stamps. And eventually my younger brother came to live with me for a while.

Q: *Turning to your professional work as a counselor, you work with many delinquents who are much like you were as an adolescent. Are you especially concerned about identifying abuse or neglect they may have experienced, or do you find it hard to keep refacing maltreatment?*

A: I think it is important to address the abuse, regardless of type, as soon as possible. As for my having to keep refacing maltreatment, it is part of my job and I am not bothered by it. Usually, I do not start out by talking about my abuse. However, when I sense it will help someone else, I do.

Q: *Of the boys enrolled in your program, what is the approximate percentage that have been physically abused, sexually abused, psychologically abused, and/or neglected?*

A: I don't know the exact percentage, but I'd say upwards of 80 percent have experienced some type of significant maltreatment.

Q: *Did most of the maltreatment they experienced occur before or after they became involved in delinquency?*

A: Mostly before.

Q: *Are the boys who have been maltreated more difficult to work with than those boys who have not been or not as severely?*

A: Yes. It's a lot harder to gain their trust. They have a lot of cynicism and very little sense of what constitutes a healthy relationship. Through positive role modeling and consistent reinforcement toward prosocial behaviors and attitudes we teach kids that success is within their reach as long as they don't give up on themselves.

Q: *Can you see ways in which their abuse directly relates to their delinquency?*

A: Crimes committed by boys who have been physically abused tend to be more aggressive. The more intense the abuse experience, the more intense their crimes tend to be.

Q: *To do effective counseling with aggressive delinquents who have been abused, do you think it's essential to have your kind of background?*

A: For whatever reason, the more aggressive kids tend to gravitate to me, and I like working with them. However, there are some residents with abuse histories who prefer professional members of our staff. What I like is the availability of staff members who have been abused, used drugs, gone through the court system, as well as those who come to work by virtue of their professional training. So to answer your question, no, I do not think it's essential.

Q: *Was it essential for you to have a therapist with an abuse history?*

A: Not necessarily abuse, but someone who had been exposed to a lot of adversity and overcome it. I particularly needed such a person during the early part of my treatment when I needed proof that people could overcome such experiences.

Q: *If you were to draw up a list of the main contributing causes of delinquency, what would your list consist of?*

A: Maltreatment, lack of nurturance, substance abusing parents, lack of appropriate limits and demands placed on you as a child, lack of positive role models, lack of direction, lack of meaning. Eventually, the peer thing becomes very important, but in almost all cases the problem originates with the parents or families. This is not to say that all parents of delinquents don't love their kids. Some do. A family should be a place where members can receive guidance, nurturance, and if all members feel this, then the likelihood of their going astray decreases.

Q: *How would you answer judges who ask whether they should look for abuse or neglect histories in delinquents' backgrounds if the courts do not have adequate resources to help maltreated adolescents?*

A: I appreciate the difficult task courts face because maltreatment is so widespread, but I think they should inquire about abuse and push to see that maltreated children and youth receive services. Everybody talks about money and that services cost too much. But what is more important than properly providing for young people? What kind of society is it that won't care for its young? I would further suggest that in addition to seeking treatment for the child, the family should be expected to seek professional help as the child can't change his family.

Q: *Do you have any recommendations as to how the juvenile justice system can better respond to maltreated delinquents?*

A: Maybe if I had received earlier intervention, I could have avoided some of the trouble I got into. Why did it take until fifth grade for me to receive special assistance? I couldn't read or write, yet I kept getting passed from one grade to the next. I wasted my first five years of education and had to go through a lot of humiliation. Similarly, the police used to arrest me but their only interest was learning who was with me. They never wanted to know about what I liked, or what was going on at home, or why I was crying. They just wanted to use me to solve a crime. In contrast, the court I was brought before did give me a good probation officer. She was instrumental in my beginning to change.

Q: *Why was she effective?*

A: She cared about me, and I felt safe with her. She talked with me, bought me an ice cream, took me shopping with her at the mall. She made me feel normal by doing normal things. I didn't feel like a punk when I was with her. She also kept reinforcing the fact that I had the potential to be someone, to do well. She stood up for me in court, first getting me removed from my home and placed in a foster home with my aunt. When this didn't work, she got me into Odyssey House. In some ways she was like a big sister that I had always wanted. Even after being placed, she visted me regularly and shared my success.

Q: *Do you have any recommendations for "systems" people who deal with delinquents?*

A: All involved systems need to communicate better with one another. For example, it doesn't help when a social worker or probation officer or police officer brings a kid to a program and then is not heard from again—unless the kid does not do well and then they want to know why, as if we've done something wrong. They have to stay involved; otherwise, the kid figures they don't care. I am also bothered by attorneys whose sole interest seems to be to get kids free of the court or anything that might help them. Treatment and/or therapy should not be viewed as a punishment.

Q: *Do you have any advice for juvenile court judges?*

A: Do your best to visit, learn about the many programs and resources available for troubled youth. Also, talk to residents on what helps them best. Face the problems the young person is experiencing, and recognize there is an important difference between punishment and treatment. Also, know what resources are available. Don't be afraid to take a chance on behalf of a kid. And be firm when it's called for. Remember that it's important to be consistent when dealing with adolescents. This shows them that you care and really want them to be successful.

Q: *Can you elaborate on punishment versus treatment?*

A: The only thing that court-ordered punishment did to me was intensify my hatred. It reinforced in my mind that the court and police were power hungry. When I was punished by being sent to jail, I used to lash out like an animal—kicking and yelling. But underneath all of this, I was scared to death and really screaming in my mind, "Why am I here? I'm sorry; I didn't mean to do it." If there was a trained counselor or social worker that could have talked with me while I was in jail, it might have helped me understand why I was so confused and angry. Sometimes a kid has to be incarcerated, but jail should only be used short-term. This sometimes forces a kid to see he's hit rock-bottom. Restitution, in my mind, is an excellent response courts can make to delinquents. If I break a window maliciously, I should pay for that window. This is not punishment. It's teaching kids to accept the consequences for their behavior. Also, there should always be a treatment option. When in court, talk to the kid. Get his thoughts, feelings, and comment on his appearance rather than just reading the progress note or talking to attorneys or workers.

Q: *Is a delinquent's history of abuse or neglect justification for some or all of his/her delinquent acts?*

A: No. Just as my parents were not justified in abusing me even though they had problems, abused kids are not justified in acting out against other persons or their property. I don't feel good about the things I did. Individuals must be held responsible for their actions. I'm just suggesting that we be more creative in our approach.

Q: *Any final thoughts about the abuse-delinquency connection?*

A: Although I received a lot of abuse and pain, I was given the opportunity to learn about these things. I like to think that, through treatment, I have been able to turn weaknesses into strengths. I'm breaking away from patterns of abuse that have been within my birth family for a long time. I am also putting roots down in areas where no one else in my family ever has although my sister is right behind me. I feel alive. I feel I have a new lease on life and this time I have no doubts about keeping up the payments. I am okay with myself. I continue to grow and learn about life.

3
A Counselor's View

Pam Hagan

P am Hagan was raised in poverty in a small southern town. Although some of her siblings became delinquents, she was always serious about school and earned a college degree in nursing. She accepted the position of program nurse at Odyssey House in New Hampshire in 1973. Following a successful training period as a counselor, she became the primary therapist for the female residents in the program who had been sexually abused. She is also a survivor, a former incest victim.

Q: *Of the delinquent girls at Odyssey House, what percentage year in and year out have been sexually abused?*

A: I haven't kept records, but over the years we have had ten to fifteen female clients in residence at any given time. Of these, I would estimate seven or eight have been sexually abused. In recent years the percentage of disclosure is higher than in the mid-1970s. Today, girls are more willing to disclose their sexual abuse since society is more open in its assessment of the problem.

Q: *What percentage involve intrafamily sexual abuse or incest?*

A: About 80 percent. When I say "intrafamily," I include father-figures such as a mother's boyfriend, uncles, grandfathers, stepfathers, in addition to biological fathers. The other 20 percent is made up of neighbors, friends of the family, and professionals such as teachers, scout leaders and camp counselors.

Q: *Does the intrafamily sexual abuse first occur prior to adolescence or during?*

A: With the girls we see, it is mostly experienced during the preadolescent period, between the ages of nine to thirteen. Some cases begin as early as age three and vary if there are other siblings in the family. It is not un-common to defer to younger children as the older child becomes resistant.

Q: *Is there any typical duration of the abuse?*

A: It's usually ongoing until the child leaves the home, often through run-ning away. Thirteen or fourteen is a common age for abused girls to take flight or seek some way to escape further abuse. In some cases it contin-ues through late adolescence, if the child remains at home.

Q: *Do the girls you have worked with typically experience other types of intrafamily maltreatment, other than sexual abuse?*

A: Yes, physical abuse and neglect, especially emotional neglect is common among the girls I see. The parent or parents are preoccupied with their jobs or personal problems and are not in tune with the needs of the child.

Q: *Is the physical abuse closely connected to the sexual abuse?*

A: Physical abuse when present usually precedes the sexual abuse. Generally, sexual abuse and physical abuse do not co-exist. It is not uncommon for the physical abuse to terminate once the sexual abuse is underway. In this sense, the physical abuse is used as bargaining strategy in exchange for the "sexual favors." The sexual abuse is physically less painful and a mild victory in the short run.

Q: *What does the physical abuse consist of?*

A: I've heard just about everything, ranging from fathers taking daughters down into the basement, tying them to posts and whipping them with belts, to slapping them around. Frequently, the beatings involve sexual exposure such as pulling the pants down.

Q: *Of the girls who are sexually abused, how many also experience emo-tional or psychological abuse?*

A: I think they go hand-in-hand. Once intrafamily sexual abuse starts, there is a lot of emotional abuse that accompanies it. This involves such things as being forbidden to tell anyone about the incest, especially the mother. That's a real emotional trauma as the child fears that disclosure will upset the family unit.

Q: *Is the emotional abuse apt to be as harmful or more harmful?*

A: Experiencing physical or sexual abuse from one's parent or care giver is a terrible dilemma from which there is no escape. It's the inability to escape that presents such an emotional burden. This is as damaging as the sexual or physical abuse. Feeling trapped is as damaging as some of the more blatant types of verbal abuse.

Q: *In addition to the intrafamily sexual abuse, how many of the delinquent girls you have seen over the years have been sexually abused outside the home?*

A: If you are talking about stranger rape or molestation, the delinquent girls I have worked with seldom have had such experiences. Most of them were first sexually abused in their homes by a family member.

Q: *What about other victimization experiences for these girls after they have left home at age thirteen or fourteen?*

A: Once the abuse has occurred in the home and the girls leave home, they are at risk for continued victimization. A high number of the girls we counsel have had such experiences. They typically select boyfriends who are six or seven years older, or ally with older males as a way of trying to find security and nurturance.

Q: *What do you make of such continuing patterns of victimization? Delinquent girls, for example, seem to put themselves in very risky positions at times, such as hitchhiking late at night or going into male hangouts. Delinquent boys often behave similarly. What are your thoughts about this?*

A: There is an element of low self-esteem, which plays a direct part in the girls putting themselves in the type of risky situations to which you refer. They are looking for a rescuer and will readily go with males who initially are nice to them. Then comes the sexual confrontation, which is much like the home situation where they were unable or not allowed to say no, and further sexual abuse results. The girls will remain in abusive situations believing that this is just the way the world is. They have fled such situations before to no avail. Like many other incest victims, delinquent girls feel soiled or damaged because of the sexual abuse, and many conclude that this is what they deserve. It becomes even easier to accept when there are secondary gains, such as drugs, a place to live, or money.

This behavior stems from the initial role confusion at home. Adults are supposed to protect and care for their children, not abuse and harm them. When abused kids get into victim or victimizing situations outside the home, they are trying to get needs met that were never met in the home. They are looking for comfort and security, not sexual gratification.

Q: *Isn't a lay person apt to think it's just crazy for an adolescent girl or boy who has been abused in the home as a child to seek out abusive situations outside of the home?*

A: Yes, but they need to understand these kids are looking for an escape, and it's hard for the kids to admit that sometimes what they run to is as bad as what they experienced at home. However, if you are on the street, where you have nothing and someone comes along with an offer to take you in, it's hard to turn it down. Then they get raped or assaulted. Many abused kids will repeat this pattern over and over; it's like a learned helplessness.

Q: *What about the role of other traumas these children experience?*

A: Among the girls I work with, it is rare to see only a single trauma. Usually, there are multiple traumas, both inside and outside the home. Divorce, parental suicide attempts, parental abandonment, multiple parental figures, psychiatric hospitalization of a parent, parental alcoholism and drug abuse are common inside the home. In fact, we see as much drug abuse by parents as by their children. This, of course, is poor role modeling, which is another negative impact.

Outside the home, many of the girls we see experience a lot of stress, particularly associated with school. Some of the girls are very bright, are not challenged, and soon become bored, act out, and get suspended. Others may be learning disabled or educationally handicapped in some way which prevents them from keeping up. A significant number have not received proper early intervention. Gradually, they fall by the wayside. This has a significant relationship to their becoming involved in delinquent behaviors.

Q: *You are suggesting a trifurcated life many of your clients experience: child abuse in the home, a variety of serious parental problems, and great difficulty in school. Do you have an opinion as to which of these three factors weighs most heavily on your clients?*

A: They are interwoven. If these kids had one sanctuary or one place where they could have a respite from all the abuse, failing, and chaos, I think they could avoid some of the more serious difficulties they later encounter. For example, if an abused child can do well in school, it's a significant offset to the abuse or family problems at home. But if you are failing at home and in school, there is a feeling of being doomed.

If I had to choose between a supportive school or supportive home environment, I'd pick the latter because the home is where one derives a basic sense of safety and security. Therefore, I would conclude that an abusive family situation is more damaging than a negative or insensitive school experience. The delinquent girls I see are in particularly bad situations because of abuse in the home, failure in school, *and* the absence of anyplace they can develop positive feelings about themselves.

Q: *Is there a central trauma most or all of these girls have experienced, or have you just expressed it?*

A: Most of what I hear from the girls is that because of their sexual abuse, they had to grow up prematurely. They had to take on the role of father's lover, caretaker for younger siblings, and frequently, manager of the household. It is not a natural role for a young girl, resulting in a great deal of pressure and confusion. They are thirteen year olds functioning or trying to function as adults. In addition, society encourages children to take on a pseudomature role. Adolescents today are preoccupied with working, buying jewelry, and wearing makeup to appear older.

Q: *Is it accurate, then, to see many delinquent girls as suffering from tremendous pressure to be adultlike at a very early age, one source being the general societal pressure you talk about and the other their being incest victims?*

A: Yes, many adolescents are left unsupervised after school and learn to make independent decisions at an early age. The loss of their childhood, i.e., time to be nurtured, is a real trauma, which often goes unnoticed until adulthood when they are expected to nurture others.

Q: *Do the girls see their victimization as meaning the same thing or are there significant differences?*

A: There are similarities, but every girl I have worked with initially feels that her sexual abuse is like no one else's. The feelings involved are of being different, alone, and sometimes even special.

Q: *Does disclosure lessen the feelings of being different and alone?*

A: Yes, for many girls it is a relief to realize others have experienced similar abuse.

Q: *What feelings commonly attend sexual abuse among juvenile delinquents?*

A: The low self-esteem, I mentioned before, is very common. Also, "Why me? Why was I picked?" Society sometimes reinforces these feelings by suggesting that female victims are at fault by virtue of putting themselves in risky situations and dressing in mature or alluring ways.

Q: *Are these feelings the same for delinquent and nondelinquent girls?*

A: I think they are. Both groups have feelings of being trapped, anger at being trapped, and great difficulty in processing these feelings.

Q: *What about guilt feelings? Are these feelings common among victims?*

A: Yes, based on a sense that they have been a willing participant. For example, it is not uncommon for an adolescent girl to test out her emerging sexuality in some flirtatious way with her father. If the father is healthy, he will handle the flirting in an appropriate manner, assuring his daughter that she is attractive but without becoming sexually entangled. If the father is unhealthy and does not control his impulses, a sexual relationship could begin that, one could say, was initiated by the young daughter. Also, there can be pleasurable feelings associated with sexual stimulation, leading to more guilt—because the girls know that a sexual relationship with a father is wrong.

Q: *It would seem that the angry feelings might be easier to deal with in therapy than the guilt feelings.*

A: The guilt feelings are usually the most difficult to come to understand. In contrast, angry feelings, which prior to therapy are usually turned against themselves, can be seen as appropriate. The girls, with therapy, can overcome both the angry and guilty feelings. The key is disclosing the incest, followed by appropriate therapeutic intervention.

Q: *How many of the girls disclosed their intrafamily sexual abuse prior to coming to Odyssey House in mid-adolescence?*

A: About half have disclosed to a case worker or probation officer. Also, in more recent years, many more of the cases have been reported to the criminal justice or child protection agency. In contrast, when I first began working with incest victims in the early and middle 1970s, state intervention was rare.

Although the increase in state intervention is good on the one hand, it also creates its own set of problems. When youth workers become privy to the incest information they must, legally, report it. As a result, the child often feels twice victimized—once by the parent, then again by the people in whom they confide. This can be very damaging. Counselors need to understand that incest victims frequently have a lot of ambivalent feelings toward their parent-perpetrator. One day the child may hate the parent, but the next day be understanding and protective toward him or her. The feelings coexist, and failure to be aware of this will result in alienating the child.

Q: *What approach should counselors take in the face of disclosed incest information?*

A: Most important is to find out why the client has chosen to disclose at this time and what she or he wants you to do with the information. Doing nothing or keeping the secret is not the thing to do. The disclosure was made for a purpose. Find out what it is.

Q: *Is it essential for the girls to disclose and talk about their abuse?*

A: Yes, as long as the abuse remains a secret, healing can not take place. When I was a young girl, disclosure was rare. You hear about adult surviviors of childhood sexual abuse disclosing years afterwards. It is far better to disclose and discuss the abuse soon after it has occurred. This allows for earlier resolution of conflict areas and reduces the likelihood of continuing victimization and/or perpetration patterns. Without disclosure, sexual abuse victims retain a secret that eats away at them and significantly affects their ability to do well in life.

Q: *Is there something that courts can do to facilitate disclosure?*

A: One thing courts could do is compile a complete child abuse history when the child first comes to the court's attention. This should be done within the context of finding out why a child is engaged in delinquent behavior and as part of an overall social history. An improperly trained intake worker is apt to elicit poor information, and it often takes two to three sessions to obtain sexual abuse data, in particular. Also, asking a young person such questions at a time when he or she is coming before the court on delinquency charges may not be the best time because so much is going on. Yet this is no reason not to ask, and the asking may prove very helpful in breaking the abuse cycle. A full assessment of each delinquent can be costly, but I believe it is money well-spent.

Q: *Would you have courts screen for sexual abuse in all female delinquency cases?*

A: Yes. Timing is critical as most victims are not apt to disclose their abuse in response to a questionnaire administered during court intake. But I think that the screening should be done, nevertheless. Also, there can be followup and the questionnaire administered a second and third time.

Q: *Should female court officials be used to administer such a questionnaire to adolescent girls, and male court officials for adolescent boys?*

A: That's the best way to do it, although it can work—sometimes better— the other way around. In a related sense, I have seen some girls do much better with male probation officers over the course of their involvement with the courts. A lot of it has to do with how bonded these kids are to mother vs. father. But, as a general rule, I think it better to use a same sex official to ask sensitive questions about sexual abuse.

Q: *What type of delinquency do the girls you counsel typically engage in?*

A: Most typical are the softer types of delinquency such as running away, truancy, drug use. It is unusual to find girls guilty of b&e's, theft and the harder types of delinquency unless they are paired with a male partner.

Q: *Does any of their delinquency involve violence?*

A: It's usually nonviolent among the girls. However, I do see considerable aggression among the girls when an authority figure, such as a police officer, attempts to restrain them. Then you get the resisting arrest and assaulting a police officer charges.

Q: *Is there a link, as you see it, between the early childhood sexual abuse and the girls' later delinquency?*

A: Given that many of the delinquent girls I work with are incest victims, I'd have to say there is a definite connection, but I work with a small population of delinquent girls. In my experience I have seen a high cor-relation between incest and running away behaviors.

Q: *What about the connection between sexual abuse and teen prostitution?*

A: I don't see a lot of blatant prostitution, the on-the-corner-selling-yourself type of situation. What I usually see is more subtle; for example, the girls engaging in sex for a meal, or for drugs. Although not a for-money ar-rangement, it is prostitution. Let me add that many of our male residents are involved in much the same type of subtle prostitution.

Q: *Do you think that delinquent boys have experienced similarly high rates of sexual abuse?*

A: Yes, although with the boys it is more extrafamily than intrafamily, in-volving scout leaders, teachers, wilderness experience counselors, and the like. Of course, this is only what they are disclosing. In fact, their rate of intrafamily incest victimization may also be high. Off the top of my head, I can think of five boys currently at Odyssey House who have been sex-ually abused, out of a total of twenty-five male residents. No doubt, there are more that I am not aware of, either because they have not disclosed or I have not consulted on their treatment.

Q: *Are the boys similarly affected by sexual abuse in terms of how they feel about it?*

A: The feelings may be similar in some respects, such as feelings of isolation and low self-esteem, but there are significant differences in disclosure. To reveal the secret, boys must not only break through the adult-child sex taboo but also the male-male taboo as the boys most often have male perpetrators. Very likely, the male-male issue causes boy victims an ad-ditional set of feelings that girl victims usually do not experience as their perpetrators are usually male. Yet another taboo that is frequently in-volved with male victimization is anal penetration. Consequently, I be-lieve that the overall impact of sexual abuse is more damaging for boys than for girls.

Q: *What fundamental differences are there, if any, in disclosure and coun-seling male victims?*

A: Certainly disclosure is more difficult because multiple taboos are in-volved. As for counseling, I believe the therapeutic process is generally the same.

Q: *How much training is required before a youth worker can responsibly counsel sexually abused delinquents, girls or boys?*

A: First of all, therapists have to be comfortable discussing this particular subject. If they are not comfortable and skirt sexual issues or use slang terms for parts of the body, then the young people they are counseling will also shy away from sexual issues. They also have to be nonjudgmental and know what their own biases are before they start counseling someone.

Q: *Does this mean that some people who are otherwise good therapists will never be comfortable with sexual issues?*

A: I think that's true. There are excellent therapists who openly admit that due to their own upbringing they are not good at dealing with this particular subject. I think it is important they acknowledge this because if they don't and attempt to counsel a sexual abuse victim, it won't be very successful.

Q: *How does a nonjudgmental approach fit in concerning the perpetrator?*

A: As I indicated before, victims are usually ambivalent about the perpetrator, especially if he or she is a family member. Negative comments by a therapist directed at the perpetrator taps into the victim's ambivalence, the love-hate aspect of the relationship, and runs the risk of driving away the victim/client.

Q: *What if the victim expresses hatred toward the perpetrator?*

A: If we are talking about a family member perpetrator, I think the therapist should maintain a neutral position. Allow the client to express the feelings of hatred and even validate that it is O.K. to have such feelings about your father, for example, but don't say, "Yes, you should hate your father," or "Your father is really a terrible person for what he has done."

Q: *How do you handle the reporting requirement with the client?*

A: As a counselor, you have to report any suspected or actual abuse. Usually, I try to involve the adolescents in the reporting process, doing it with the victim so that she does not feel that I am doing something behind her back. Many times, victims want the abuse reported, not necessarily for criminal prosecution but as an additional way of ensuring that the abuse is terminated.

Q: *What is your feeling about criminal prosecutions against perpetrators, especially intrafamily perpetrators?*

A: My feeling is that the court procedure is drawn out over a long period of time, and sometimes the court procedures are as traumatic as the original abuse. The victim has to re-live all of the abuse. If the court process could run its course more quickly, there would be less trauma to the victims who have to live with anxiety over sending a father, brother, or uncle to prison. And they really don't want to disrupt the family. Victims sometimes are pressured by other family members not to testify, making them feel even more guilty. So it is a very tough thing to go through.

Q: *What are your basic principles in being a therapist for sexually abused delinquent girls?*

A: A therapist has to honestly assess whether this is the type of issue he or she feels comfortable dealing with. For example, for a long time I could not work with perpetrators due to my own incest victimization. I limited myself to working with victims because I felt comfortable doing this. Only in recent years have I come to feel comfortable working with perpetrators. More than anything, I think the key is working out one's own hangups and biases and being able to listen objectively.

Q: *So you feel that abuse histories need to be uncovered and addressed therapeutically?*

A: Yes, when kids come before courts for delinquency, we need to find out what is going on. I firmly believe that few kids are born bad. Something turns them the wrong way, and we need to find out what it is in each case.

Q: *What is the likely effect of abused delinquents not being counseled about their abuse, be it sexual or some other type of abuse?*

A: Generally, you'll see victims going through life with poor social skills, mistrust of authority figures, low self-esteem, depression, sometimes guilt, and a lot of misdirected anger, which is an element in a lot of delinquency and crime.

Q: *Are there other types of effective responses other than traditional one-to-one or group therapy?*

A: Group therapy is the treatment modality of choice for sexual abuse victims. Initially, there usually has to be a one to one counseling arrangement because adolescents are hesitant about disclosing sexual abuse in a group setting. After disclosure, victims can derive a great deal of compassion and support from other victims through the group process. For persons who are blocked and just cannot talk about traumatic childhood experiences, there are such things as expressive therapy through art or writing that have been very effective.

Q: *Is group work equally effective for delinquent boys who have been sexually abused? Isn't there a macho element that makes group work risky?*

A: Yes, I think there are greater difficulties with male victims, and, consequently, one to one counseling may have to be used for a longer period of time at the outset of treatment. The group process has a lot to offer and should be used whenever possible.

Q: *What about the value of, say, an outward bound-type experience for abuse victims?*

A: There can be value to this kind of experience, particularly in offering opportunities to exert oneself physically and take out aggression in a healthy way. In a similar sense, being employed as a manual laborer can be a healthy outlet. But these are short-range methods that allow for positive expression of some surplus aggression. Eventually, the abuse has to be talked about and processed therapeutically.

Q: *Given today's knowledge that so many delinquents have abuse histories, you'd agree that counselors serving adolescent clients need to have some basic training in maltreatment issues?*

A: Yes. They have to be familiar with such basics as perpetrator dynamics and the different strategies perpetrators use to engage victims. A counselor's lack of knowledge about these and similar fundamentals is discouraging to victim/clients.

Q: *Does a person have to have been a victim in order to be a successful sexual abuse counselor?*

A: Not having been a victim can be used by victims against a counselor, but I see this as just another excuse for the client not facing up to the abuse. Of course, if the counselor has also been a victim, this can be an advantage. But it certainly is not a prerequisite for being a good sexual abuse counselor. In my situation, I do not always immediately disclose my abuse experience to the adolescent client unless it's necessary. I don't like to use my abuse as an initial engagement strategy because then the client is apt to say, "Well, you know what it's like," and clams up. I am also careful how I share my abuse experience because I do not want to suggest to the girls who I am counseling that nonvictim counselors will not be able to help them. In fact, they can, and I do not want to foreclose this option. Let me add that I think it can be very useful for nonvictim counselors to invite adult survivors to group sessions, especially survivors who have become successful in several roles.

Q: *You are a wife, mother, trained nurse, counselor, and former victim. How do the girls you counsel mainly see you?*

A: I think they see me in all of these roles, which is good because they can see, notwithstanding my own victimization, that it is possible to have a positive family life. They can also see it is possible to do productive work, to move beyond the victimization and not be trapped for life by it. It's encouraging to them.

Q: *You have siblings who became delinquent, others who experienced considerable academic and job success. How do you account for the different outcomes?*

A: In my family, the boys became delinquent and the girls were able to attain some success, thereby avoiding delinquency. None of the boys have had any therapeutic intervention. They've rebelled against counseling. It seems to threaten their ego. In contrast, all three of my sisters have been in therapy to talk about the abuse, to process it.

Q: *Is there a common denominator among abused delinquent girls who benefit from therapy and go on to a better life?*

A: I think it is the relief derived from disclosing the abuse, and the subsequent knowledge that they are not alone and that they did not do anything wrong.

Q: *If the nation's juvenile court judges were to ask you the best way to respond to female delinquents, what would your answer be?*

A: To treat them as seriously as male delinquents, even though their crimes are usually less serious than the boys'. The girls' being in juvenile court is equally significant. My concern is that whereas boys often receive supportive intervention on the basis of their offenses being serious, girls often do not receive the benefit of such intervention because their delinquency is not considered as offensive. My belief is that truancy and running away for a girl are as deviant as b&e's for boys. Early, effective intervention is the key and girls are not helped when they are released with little or no court intervention.

Q: *What about the role of punishment, such as sentencing to reform school?*

A: Punishment, in my view, is rarely productive with these kids. However, I also believe that you have to pay for what you do. If you break the law, you should pay the consequences. Restitution satisfies this for me, in many cases. This is in contrast to pure punishment which, when administered to already mistrustful kids, leads to feelings of humiliation and more anger. It just reinforces their low self-esteem. We need to keep in mind, too, that the abused delinquent has been "punished" all of his or her life. And punishment can be the easy way out for a lot of kids because there is no requirement that they confront what is really bothering them and fueling their delinquency.

Q: *Should any kind of distinctions be made between male and female delinquents in terms of court handling?*

A: None. Juvenile courts tend to be paternalistic toward girls, too easy. A girl pins a ribbon in her hair the day of court, puts on a sweet smile, and the judge lets her off. There is, consequently, less justice where girls are concerned.

Q: *How do you answer court officials who ask, "Should we screen for abuse if we don't have the resources to commit to victims who disclose?"*

A: I think it's wrong not to ask. If only one adolescent out of ten or twenty discloses, you have a clue about the connection to delinquency. Once disclosure is made, there is an obligation to create or develop resources to meet the child's needs.

Q: *Has too much damage been done to the girls by the time they enter the juvenile justice system in early or midadolescence?*

A: No, adolescence is a prime intervention time because, in some ways, youths within this age/time range are better able to respond to therapeutic treatment than preadolescents.

Q: *Once a court has ordered therapeutic intervention, what is a reasonable expectation of a delinquent, generally speaking?*

A: It's not always steady, upward progress. There is a lot of "two-steps forward-and-one-back" with these kids. Also, it is unrealistic to expect these young people to be "cured" after even a year or more of intensive treatment. They still have to face their home situation, old peers, and their home community where negativity abounds. One key is for courts to insist on parental involvement whenever possible, so that the family is making some adjustments at the same time the young people are.

Q: *Probation officers are key people in working with delinquents, male and female. How can probation officers best help their young charges?*

A: Probation officers should find out what their clients' main problems are and advocate in such a way that those problem areas are addressed. They also can help kids to sort out what is happening to them. It's a tough job as delinquents often view probation officers as simply people who have to accept their assignments and who do not care about them personally. It takes a good probation officer to see beyond this defensiveness and develop a rapport with the kids.

Q: *Is it fair to say that if you could magically erase the abuse factor in female delinquents' lives—the physical and sexual abuse, the emotional barrages, and the neglect—that the majority of these girls would not wind up before juvenile courts?*

A: I think that's fair to say. I have seen very few girls come to Odyssey House during my time, which goes back to the early 1970s, who have not experienced some type of serious maltreatment. It is the maltreatment that links to their feelings about themselves more than anything else and these feelings, in turn, link to their delinquency.

Q: *But presumably, their lives would not be perfect and there would still be parent-child problems?*

A: That's right. But such things as divorce and parental alcoholism are more workable than child abuse. Children can handle divorce; they can handle a parent's drinking; but child abuse particularly when combined with these other factors, which it often is with our girls—is too much. Also, child abuse triggers feelings within a child that are more intense than feelings a child usually gets from other traumas.

Q: *You were abused as a child and you did not become delinquent. So presumably, there are factors at work in shaping delinquency other than sexual abuse as a child?*

A: Yes. In my case, school was my salvation. I did well in school. I couldn't wait to get to school. By doing well at school, I got positive reinforcement from teachers and guidance counselors. School became my sanctuary and the reason I survived all of my abuse. Some kids, however, can't find anything to be good at, something to feel good about. They are the ones who never get any positive attention and praise.

Q: *Did you receive praise at home for doing well in school?*

A: No. What I got was a reprieve from being beaten. The other children in my family who did not do well at school were beaten and verbally abused. Because they did poorly in school, my siblings were frequently truant and that gave them time to get into "trouble."

Q: *What would have happened if you had not had school as an outlet?*

A: I would have had more problems, no doubt. Although I was never brought before a court, I was not entirely problem-free. I ran away from home several times to escape the abuse, but my father always brought me back home. Also, I think that I had some innate characteristics that helped me endure the incest.

Q: *So you believe that inherited factors, genes or whatever, play some part in explaining why some abused children cope better with maltreatment than other abused children?*

A: Yes. This, coupled with one area of my life being positive—schooling—is what made the difference in my case.

Q: *What are the other ingredients for abused delinquents becoming successful? You've cited the essential need for them to disclose and talk about the abuse. What else is involved, and how do you proceed given that these young people typically have so many problems?*

A: School is a key. More teachers and other school personnel need training in child abuse basics to facilitate more disclosure. I also see a need for more hands-on opportunities for these children—cooking, industrial arts. Classes in coping skills would help a lot, as would classes on such things as alcoholism and sexual abuse. Such things are beginning to be done, but we need to do more.

Q: *Do these young people have to obtain some measure of educational success if they are to make it?*

A: I'm not sure all of them have to, but school is very important to young people and those who don't make it are in a tough position. Some of the kids at Odyssey House just weren't able to function in the public schools but have blossomed at our school. We have one boy who was illiterate when he came to us at fifteen. He required a lot of one-to-one attention. He now takes delight in reading. Our teachers do an incredible job. It's astonishing to observe the changes.

Q: *Any final thoughts about the abuse-delinquency connection?*

A: Because there have been very few girls at Odyssey House over the years who have not experienced some type of maltreatment, I feel there is a clearcut connection between the abuse and the girls' delinquency. I do not believe kids are predestined to a life of delinquency. They become angry because of what is done to them, and in turn, the anger links to the delinquency.

4

A Psychiatrist's View

Rowen Hochstedler

Rowen Hochstedler is a psychiatrist who first began to work with delinquents in 1970 as director of Odyssey House New York's Adolescent Unit. Thereafter, he was psychiatric consultant to Odyssey House New Hampshire for fifteen years. Currently, he is in private practice in Massachusetts and continues to consult to agencies that serve delinquents and abused children.

Q: *Over the years, you have interviewed, counseled, and guided the therapy of hundreds of delinquents, many with abuse histories. Based on your experience, can you give us some initial observations about abused delinquents?*

A: An important first step is simply to ask delinquents about a possible history of abuse. Frequently, however, abuse has to be uncovered over a period of time, often in the context of an intense therapeutic relationship.

Second, there are a number of clues that lead one to suspect abuse. Aggressive behavior with a great deal of underlying anger is always a symptom that should lead one to suspect abuse.

Third, one should always keep in mind that abused youth will respond to their abuse on the basis of their own unique personality style. In almost all cases the abuse experience is damaging, and the abuse is a major factor in their delinquency.

Q: *Is there a significant difference in prognosis for abused versus nonabused delinquents?*

A: Follow-up studies indicate that the prognosis for delinquents, regardless of abuse, is not very good. To my knowledge, none of these studies considers the abuse factor. Our experience in psychiatric practice is that the presence of abuse, in delinquent or other patient populations, makes the prognosis less favorable.

Q: *Have you seen an increase in the number of male victims of sexual abuse?*

A: Yes. We don't know is whether there are actually more males being sexually abused or whether it is now easier for males to disclose abuse in the mid-1980s.

Q: *What are the treatment goals for abused delinquents?*

A: The foremost treatment goal for all delinquents is to be able to live in society in a lawful manner. In my opinion abused delinquents must be treated, in one way or another, for a period of years. Abuse cannot be treated within a short-term framework.

Q: *Which methodologies do you prefer?*

A: That is an important question because there is growing controversy over various methodologies. I have already indicated my belief that whatever the treatment methodology, it needs to be long-term. High intensity, short-term approaches, in my view, do not work. Beyond this, I think that each abuse case has to be handled on an individual basis, depending on the nature of the abuse and the particular victim involved.

Certainly, homogeneous treatment groups for adolescents can be beneficial, but for the long haul, I prefer an individualized approach. This individualized treatment program should be based on the personality, family support structure, and associated psychopathology of the delinquent. Even an abused adolescent who has completed a treatment program at age sixteen has not necessarily put the abuse issue to rest. Over the years at Odyssey House, for example, we have seen how the abuse damage became reactivated at critical life junctures such as marriage or having a child of one's own.

Mention should also be made of pharmacologic treatments for impulsive, aggressive adolescents. I believe that such treatments may be effective for the treatment of specific symptoms but should be used only in the context of a larger therapy program.

Q: *Does this mean that one-to-one or individual therapy will be essential at some point for abused delinquents?*

A: In the later stages of treatment, yes. Initially, delinquents are extremely difficult to engage in conventional one-to-one therapy, and, therefore, the group process is an indispensable tool.

Q: *Are there significant differences in rehabilitative methods for girls versus boys?*

A: At Odyssey House we found that the girls were much more responsive to group therapy as a place to disclose abuse. In contrast, the boys usually disclosed in one-to-one therapy but were unable to do so until they had had considerable group therapy experience.

Q: *Increasing attention is being given to abused delinquents as adolescent perpetrators of abuse. How widespread is this in your experience, and what is the preferred method of treatment?*

A: I'm not sure how widespread this phenomenon is. What I can say is that I have yet to evaluate an adolescent perpetrator who was not, himself, an abuse victim. On the other hand, many abuse victims do not go on to become perpetrators. One perpetrator can, of course, victimize many children.

As for a preferred method of treatment, I think that almost all of these young perpetrators need to be in a highly structured program where their behavior is monitored very closely. Beyond this, I think that it is too early to tell which specific treatment strategies work best.

Incidentally, perpetrators of sexual abuse sometimes begin to victimize in preadolescence.

Q: *What is your advice to juvenile courts insofar as processing delinquents, responding to the abuse factor, and reducing the chances of recidivism?*

A: Courts need to see that careful assessments are done, and they usually need professional expertise to do these assessments. Only after collecting a substantial amount of information about an individual are they in a position to make an informed prescription. For abused delinquents, intensive therapy is usually needed. Most often, this means structured, residential treatment programs.

Courts also have the ability to encourage or compel significant persons in a delinquent's life to become involved with the treatment process. Courts can help, additionally, by clearly establishing the terms of a young person's treatment, probation, and so forth. It is very helpful to patient and therapist, alike, to know the patient's legal reality.

Q: *We have put together two delinquency cases—Laura and Mark—for you to comment on. These are not their real names nor are they actual cases, although the experienced eye will see elements of these two young people in many delinquents. Recognizing that the summary profiles only provide you with a limited amount of information, we will nevertheless ask you to assess these cases within an abuse-delinquency framework.*

Summary Profile—Laura

1. Laura was raised by her biological parents in a neglectful environment until she was three, when she was sent to live with her grandmother who resided in the same town.

2. When Laura was seven, her beloved grandmother died, and Laura returned to her biological parents.

3. From ages eight to ten, Laura's father sexually abused her. The abuse included touching, fondling, fellatio, and intercourse. Laura's mother worked part-time and spent much of her "free" time away from home as a volunteer in a service organization.

4. Laura began to shoplift (age eleven), to abuse alcohol and drugs to the point of unconsciousness (age twelve), and to prostitute with older boys and men (age thirteen). She also slashed her wrists on numerous occasions and was raped while hitchhiking.

5. Despite having above average intelligence, Laura was truant for most of her teen years. She was also in juvenile court numerous times for shoplifting, possession of drugs, being drunk and disorderly, resisting arrest, and for CHINS offenses.

Q: *Given the presence of numerous, potentially harmful family dynamics, how is it possible to assign causative weight to Laura's three-year incest experience?*

A: From a psychiatric point of view *cause and effect* can have a number of different meanings. Very rarely do we actually use the term *cause* because common use would indicate this to mean some kind of logical or physical relationship. In psychiatry we speak instead of (1) reactive conditions, (2) personality formation, (3) ego deficits and (4) genetic influences. Using these terms, one can postulate a number of relationships between Laura's experiences and the development of an antisocial pattern of behavior.

First, we look at the time sequence. Incest was carried on during a period of life that we call latency. This is a period that is ordinarily not a highly disruptive stage in a child's life, at least in lives of children who have nonviolent, caring relationships with their parents. In Laura's case, there was a set of traumatic experiences during the latency period, followed within a year or two by antisocial, aggressive behavior. For example, the incest ended at age ten, and at eleven she began to shoplift and at twelve she was abusing alcohol and drugs. It is this time element that makes, from a psychiatric point of view, a persuasive argument that the incest in Laura's case was a causative factor in the sense that the antisocial behavior is a symptom complex developed in reaction to the traumatic incest experience. I should add that voluntary patterns of behavior, such as repeated antisocial acts, are not usually seen as psychological symptoms. However, children and adolescents have a relatively restricted range of behaviors to indicate psychological distress. Therefore, with these age groups, we would consider antisocial behavior, for instance, fire setting, as a symptom of underlying psychological disturbance.

Second, we would say that Laura's personality formation was influenced by the incest experience. Instead of a quiet, supported latency, she had a stimulated, sexualized one. We would expect her personality to be dramatic, confused, and untrusting, similar to the borderline features often found in personality disorders.

Third, the ego psychologists would call the incest experience damaging in the sense of producing impairment of ego functions—sense of self, ability to differentiate appropriate from inappropriate sexual impulse, and so forth.

I also note that during the incest, Laura's mother was frequently away from home, and the question arises of what effect this neglect had on Laura's subsequent disorder. Laura may not have had any female role models at this time. In addition, there may have been genetic influences predisposing her to develop her delinquency.

In light of the complicated interplay of these various factors, I think it is impossible to assign specific causation weight to the incest.

It makes the most sense to say the following: Here is a child who is aggressively traumatized due to incest; the incest took place in an atmosphere of emotional neglect by the mother; and the combination of the incest and the neglect plus an emerging period of physical and emotional turmoil (adolescence) plus consequent emotional lability is the picture of the onset of aggressive, antisocial behavior.

Q: *Empirical scientists say that the only way to really know something about causation is to do a formal measurement with control groups, the point being that making judgments about how abuse causes delinquency is futile until the incidence of abuse among nondelinquent adolescents is known. Here, we are attempting to stimulate specific psychiatric commentary on the relationships between child abuse and delinquency for a variety of purposes other than "proving" cause-effect. Isn't it true that psychiatry is generally not concerned with one-to-one causal relationships?*

A: That's basically correct. In fact, most reasoned psychiatric opinion puts things together only in terms of time relationships. Generally, efforts that have been made to show cause-effect, psychiatrically speaking, without including time relationships have subsequently been disproven.

Thus, where there is a fairly tight time structure between events, psychiatrists are inclined to consider cause-effect phenomenon. For example, if you have an automobile accident and shortly thereafter you become depressed, that's awfully good evidence that a causal relationship exists. How are you going to prove this? One can't because many people have accidents who don't get depressed. Now, in Laura's case, the trauma occurred over a period of years, followed within a year or two by deviant behavior. As a psychiatrist I would assume that the trauma, including the incest, was causative in the terms listed above.

Q: *The initial three-year period of Laura's life must have been very difficult given that her biological parents were neglectful and sent (or were made to send) Laura to her grandmother. Wasn't this experience such that Laura was apt to feel pretty bad about herself, sufficient to have led to her later delinquent behavior?*

A: This is a type of question that provokes a great deal of controversy within the field of psychiatry. Some psychiatrists hold that the first three, four, or five years of life are critical years and everything that happens thereafter is relatively insignificant. For example, in Laura's case, she was essentially abandoned by her biological parents at age three. This may have been traumatic to Laura, although we don't know this for a fact. However, I am not inclined to believe that their abandonment of Laura inevitably led to her antisocial behavior some eight years later, and that intervening experiences could not have ameliorated any negative effects from her initial three-year period.

Q: *Although the reason for Laura's parents sending her to live with her grandmother is not known, would she be apt to perceive this as abandonment even if they did it for the best of reasons?*

A: Yes.

Q: *The prostituting in her early teens stands out as a particularly devastating effect. Would you link this extreme behavior with the incest?*

A: I think that's a very safe assumption. Although I have no outside substantiation, I think that an incest victim often cannot differentiate between nurturance, violence, and sexuality. Over the period of time, the child loses the ability to differentiate between what may be appropriate experiences of these three phenomenon and what are clearly inappropriate ones. When the female incest victim reaches the early teen years and begins to have strong sexual impulses, one can easily see that the dynamics of prostitution might emerge. She may look to the prostitution to satisfy a need for nurturance. She may also identify it more in terms of hostility because she is making the men pay for what they want.

One can see how the incest might cause confusion and can lead someone such as Laura to prostitution, although it needs to be noted that incest victims respond in other ways, including frigidity and staying away from men altogether. But in Laura's case, the kind of confusion I am talking about is likely the paramount issue leading her to seek nurturance through sex and violence. Similar dynamics appear to be operating when female incest victims become promiscuous, often becoming involved with unsavory males who abuse them.

Q: *This seems a particularly important point. Can you elaborate on this confusion?*

A: It is very important to healthy ego development to be able to have clear boundaries between certain aspects of one's behavior during one's growing-up years. For example, a child needs to know the difference between love and punishment and that punishment, at times, can be a form of love. But when a child is nurtured one minute, physically abused the next minute, and then sexualized, the child's ability to distinguish among these three becomes impaired. As the child grows up, he or she may be nontrusting toward another person's attempt to nurture, but receptive to abuse on the basis of confusing it with nurturance or caring. Sexually speaking, love-making may be viewed a hostile act. Thus, many aspects of intimacy in human relationships are confused for some abuse victims.

Q: *Is there an element of violence in Laura's relationship with her father?*

A: Although the information we have does not indicate any overt threats or actual violence, I find it difficult to imagine the incest was carried out without some threat. The father had to keep it a secret, and we know that children rarely keep such secrets because they want to. Rather, they are afraid to reveal the situation because of what the perpetrator tells them.

Q: *Then, in your mind, Laura's prostitution can be directly linked to the incest versus the other trauma such as the neglect in early childhood and death of the grandmother?*

A: Well, it's hard to say, once again, that A definitely caused B. For example, we have the second abandonment by the biological mother once Laura returned to her home following the death of her grandmother, and it certainly didn't help that Laura apparently did not have her mother around to show her how to be a normal sexual person.

Q: *Is adolescent prostitution symptomatic of especially negative feelings about self, more so than drug use or theft, for example?*

A: I think the prostitution is more deviant. This is particularly the case for young people living in suburban or rural areas versus inner city areas where prostitution is common. I think the prostitution contains in it the elements of violence, sex, and even nurturing, as I mentioned before. And yes, I think that the prostitution is definitely indicative of especially hostile feelings toward self and others.

Q: *A related question is whether Laura's selection of older men as sexual partners is significant in terms of understanding causes of her sexual acting out and possible linkage with the incest?*

A: It is tempting to make a one-to-one correlation like that, Laura selecting a father figure to repeat the incest experience, which, as bad as it was, may have been the only attentive experience she ever had with a parental figure, aside from the four years with her grandmother. However, I don't know how far you can go with that, and such line of reasoning is probably simplistic. I think it is more interesting to see what type of partners people such as Laura eventually select for the long-term future.

Q: *Laura lost her grandmother when she was seven, and the incest began when she was eight. What significance do you make of this?*

A: Her sudden death was most likely viewed, at least partially, by Laura as abandonment, followed shortly thereafter by this raw exposure to her father. A child does not have an infinite capacity to believe that the adult controlled world is filled with hope and promise. By the time of the onset of the incest, Laura had suffered through three major abandonments by: first, the biological parents when she was three, second, her grandmother when she was seven, and third, her unavailable mother when she returned to the biological home.

It would be reasonable to say that following her grandmother's death, Laura was in a vulnerable position as to trust and belief in adults. A sensitive, caring response to this condition might have done much to ameliorate these feelings. But to experience, as Laura did, incest with the father and emotional neglect by the mother could only serve to intensify the lack of trust and leave her pretty much in a state of total disillusionment. I should add that I am using the term *neglect* loosely, although there is no question that the mother's absence here is a significant matter.

Q: *You indicate that Laura's mother's unavailability had the probable effect of allowing the incest to continue, making Laura feel isolated and hopeless, and leaving Laura to seek out peers engaged in destructive activity. Such an "absent" mother figure is common in incest cases. Do you think that some of the rage that is common to abused adolescents can be attributed to this?*

A: Once again, I don't know if we have substantiation from other psychiatric sources on this, but one of the dynamics we see over and over in treatment is that some of the initial rage is directed at the perpetrator of the violence. This is understandable. But as we work with these young people in therapy, they begin to wonder about the person who should have been there to protect them. The rage then begins to become less focused on the "sick" parent and more on the "healthy" parent who didn't step in. During the course of treatment, a victim can almost forgive someone for their pathology but not for failure to intercede when the person was capable of doing so.

Q: *Young adolescents such as Laura who get caught up in violence, drugs, and sex at a very early age often are extremely cynical. Is extremely the product of the incest—i.e., does the incest result in a depth of powerful feelings that otherwise young people such as Laura might not have experienced? If yes, can any of their antisocial behavior be attributed to such feelings additionally felt?*

A: Young people who have no possibility of forming an idea of what they can become, other than being a tool for some pathological adult's pleasure, often are very cynical. Young girls such as Laura cannot see themselves as emerging women because they have had no healthy female role models to follow. The incest experience, in my view, even more than physical abuse, strikes at the child's sense of self and renders them able to see interpersonal relationships only in terms of some bit of fleeting pleasures or perhaps fragmentary gains that we probably do not understand.

Q: *Then you are saying there is probably something special or unique about Laura's incest versus the earlier abandonment experiences.*

A: I think so. Violating the sexual development process cuts more to the core of a woman's ability to feel good about herself than, say, physical abuse.

Q: *In looking at Laura's teen years (the effect years), can you see any behaviors in which hostile or cynical feelings may have been sublimated?*

A: Somewhat in the prostitution, the suicidal gestures, and some of the other dangerous behaviors such as hitchhiking, which certainly for a young girl is tantamount to setting one's self up to be raped. All of these are quite pathological.

Q: *Returning to your earlier statement about the incest destroying a young victim's trust in adults, is it accurate to describe a causal chain, psychiatrically speaking, between Laura's need to be loved and protected by her parents, their failure to meet this need, and Laura's subsequent powerful feelings, including possible guilt and rage? Might this be the chain in all abuse cases, with the primary difference being the variety of ways abused children respond to these feelings?*

A: Yes. A child can be seen as totally trusting. That trust gets violated, and the child then feels a set of powerful feelings that she is not able to assess. The child is devastated because of having no clearly felt sense of self, and she is unable to turn to someone and say, "Please take care of these feelings."

Q: *Isn't it true that children like Laura will express these feelings outwardly or inwardly on themselves or perhaps a combination of the two, and that the goal of therapy is to provide a constructive outlet for these feelings? Thus, some children with Laura's experiences might become withdrawn and self-destructive without exhibiting any outward expressions such as Laura did with the prostitution and theft.*

A: Yes. Maybe it's a gross oversimplification to talk about outward versus inward expressions of deeply felt feelings, yet I think that it can be useful to think in those terms. When a young person such as Laura begins to evidence the prostitution, wrist-slashing, and putting herself in dangerous situations, I think you have to consider that the home may have been so pathological that something like incest may have taken place.

Q: *How significant are guilt and rage in Laura's subsequent antisocial behavior?*

A: We certainly think that rage is central to the antisocial behavior. As for the guilt, we can only speculate that it was present and part of the feeling that pulled her toward self-destructive behavior. Without the guilt, Laura most likely would have been sociopathic-like, venting rage only at others, not turning it in toward herself through wrist-slashing and that type of behavior.

Q: *Isn't it also true that delinquent females typically exhibit less outward aggression than their male counterparts?*

A: Yes.

Q: *Why would victims such as Laura feel guilt?*

A: We assume in most incest processes that the victim is not wholly coerced, that is that victims are enticed, rather than subjected by physical force, and that some nurturance is derived by the victim, however distorted the nurturance may be. In this sense, victims such as Laura are willing participants and they will always have to live with this. This causes great guilt, especially when victims reach their teen years and realize the incest is wrong.

Q: *Then if Laura had been brutally raped by her father rather than enticed, cajoled, bribed, seduced, etc., she may have fared better in the sense that she may not have felt guilt in later years?*

A: Certainly. Participation can pull one into a different psychological process than total victimization. If a person is brutally raped outside the context of a parental relationship, the victim will certainly have scars but not to the extent of Laura's. A rape occurring outside the family allows the perpetrator to be viewed by the child as just an attacker. Rape by a family member is more complicating in terms of the confused feelings of the victim, because there are other aspects, presumably positive ones, to the relationship. Most damaging I believe, is repeated, noncoerced incest, because in this case all the feelings are confused.

Q: *How do you interpret Laura's extensive alcohol and drug abuse? Would she likely have been a substance abuser absent the incest?*

A: Yes, very likely. I think that the depth and severity of Laura's deviant behavior are factors linked to the incest.

Q: *You mean her frequent drinking to the point of being unconscious?*

A: Exactly.

Q: *Is this, then, an especially compelling characteristic or feature of the child abuse–delinquency connection?*

A: Yes.

Q: *How do you interpret the suicide attempt or gesture? Would she have done this if she had not been abused?*

A: Suicide gestures among adolescents are not unusual. However, when it takes place within the context that Laura's did—associated with the excessive substance abuse and sexual behavior—one is certainly tempted to make that one-to-one connection. In other words, abusing alcohol in the extremely reckless manner that she did as well as engaging in prostitution, which features a high risk of personal danger, suggest the presence of a major disturbance within someone such as Laura. Certainly incest, more so than the other dynamics in her life, can be most positively linked to such disturbance.

Q: *Aside from the prostitution, Laura engaged in five specific delinquent behaviors: possession and use of substances, being drunk and disorderly, resisting arrest, prostitution, and shoplifting. Are these specific behaviors consistent with her background, and is it surprising that she was not involved in additional kinds of delinquency?*

A: By additional kinds of delinquency, do you you mean behaviors that are less apt to result in apprehension as against those that are, such as vandalism and b&e's?

Q: *This distinction was not intended, but now that you make the point, it is a useful way to pursue this.*

A: I'm not sure young children make these kind of distinctions, or any of the ones that legal systems do, between different kinds of behaviors. I think Laura probably did what she felt she needed to do to take care of whatever feelings she was confronted with. Whether this might have included b&e's or vandalism is not a significant issue. Laura's behavior is as significant to me as the young person who does twenty b&e's and would be more apt to be considered a serious juvenile offender.

Q: *Why?*

A: Because Laura's behaviors contain rage, using other people as objects, and self-destruction. Compare this with another youth who does a b&e

to obtain money to buy drugs. Laura's behavior might well be more serious, psychiatrically speaking.

Q: *Can you elaborate on this point?*

A: Laura's behavior indicates deep-seated problems that go to the core of her being. Absent intensive therapy, she is apt to be problem laden for the remainder of her life. On the other hand, a young person who is primarily behaviorally disturbed can respond more readily to intervention as long as the antisocial behavior has not become fused with the sense of self. We have a reasonably good chance of getting these people to discontinue their illegal behaviors.

Q: *Can it be said with any psychiatric certainty that one or more of Laura's five delinquent behaviors would not have occurred if she had not been abused by her father? If not, what can be said, with some degree of certainty, about her incest and what significance might this have for courts that routinely see adolescent girls like Laura?*

A: Although it certainly would be useful to know more about Laura's social context, I believe that it is unlikely that Laura would have engaged in prostitution absent significant sexual psychopathology on the part of her family. I would also point to the severity of her self-destructive behavior—the wrist-slashing, drinking to the point of unconsciousness. The two sets of behavior together stand out as indicators of that terrible mixture of violence, sex, and nurturance. For Laura, they seemed to have been lumped together without her being able to differentiate between them. Again, this is not to say that incest directly caused or led to these behaviors. Rather, I'm saying from a psychiatric point-of-view, that when I see these specific kinds of behavior, I begin to think there very probably was abnormal sexual activity within the home involving a parent or parent-substitutes.

Q: *Is Laura's abuse experience qualitatively different from her other negative parent-child experiences? Is she uniquely affected by the incest?*

A: I think so. Going back to the confusion regarding sex, violence, and nurturance, I am not sure if someone like Laura will ever be able to get them clearly sorted out. It would not be unusual for a person like Laura to continue some confusion, a great deal of anxiety, and perhaps some ongoing acting-out behavior. I think it should be said that even intensive therapy may not enable incest victims to effectively untangle the three phenomena, but that therapy may enable someone such as Laura to reduce the severity of any acting-out or self-destructive behavior. Whether these victims can enter into successful long-term heterosexual relationships, even with the benefit of therapy, is an open question.

Q: *Are you saying that people like Laura are especially vulnerable to ongoing destructive relationships with males?*

A: Yes.

Q: *And if we could magically erase Laura's three-year incest experience, would her prospects be improved?*

A: You can never answer this kind of question 100 percent. If she had not had the incest experience and if she had had a mother who stepped in to help in times of difficulty, it is hard to imagine that Laura would have gotten into as much difficulty as she has.

Q: *What if all else were the same except that Laura's father had avoided her rather than commit incest?*

A: I'm sure she still would have had problems. However, the incest represents a boundary. Once you cross that line, it never quite gets repaired. Feelings are triggered that nonvictims don't experience.

Q: *Might there be a similar boundary line in physical abuse cases?*

A: I think so. The line, however, is somewhat different. With physical abuse, violence and nurturance get mixed up in the child. With incest, a third element is present—sex. However, in both types of abuse, I believe a special set of effects result that involve the child's developing very intense feelings of rage, love, and guilt. These feelings are apt to be overwhelming to the child, to an extent that is far less common with delinquents and others who have not been abused.

Q: *Generally speaking, how significant a factor are these "very intense feelings" in the rehabilitative process? Does this factor make intervention much more difficult than with nonabused delinquents?*

A: Very significant, mainly because people like Laura have a great deal of difficulty in compartmentalizing these feelings even with the benefit of therapy. And, yes, intervention is much more difficult.

Q: *What is an appropriate court disposition for someone such as Laura?*

A: Laura needs a chance. She needs to be removed from situations where she either repeats the pattern of self-mutilation or expresses her rage through prostitution or other means. To me, this means she needs the safety and structure of a residential program. More than this, she needs a residential program with experience treating incest victims.

Q: *In looking for hopeful signs, how significant is the four-year hiatus with the grandmother and the fact that Laura is bright?*

A: Assuming her brightness includes insight and the ability to verbalize, her intelligence is very significant. Her relationship with her grandmother is also very significant; it can serve as a model for Laura of what a healthy relationship feels like.

Q: *In terms of treatment and rehabilitation, what is reasonable expectation for the Lauras of the world?*

A: I believe that it is reasonable for the Lauras of the world to stop behaving in self-destructive ways. I think it is also reasonable for them to attain some measure of educational success. The foremost problem will be continuing difficulty with enduring, intimate relationships. They will probably need to be in and out of therapy over the years to address this.

Q: *What is the likely impact of incarceration or punishment on someone like Laura?*

A: Probably two things. First, she would likely become extremely cynical because she would experience the state as an abusive actor in her life. Second, incarceration would put her in contact with other persons who would perpetuate her illness.

Summary Profile—Mark

1. At birth, Mark was turned over by his parents to be raised by his aunt and uncle. Because of "overcrowding" in the family, after he was five, Mark was placed in a foster home where he remained until he was nine. While at the foster home, his foster mother would often punish him for poor behavior by making him wear a dress. She also beat him with a hairbrush.
2. At nine, Mark was returned to his aunt and uncle, and soon thereafter his alcoholic uncle began to beat him. The physical abuse included kick-

ing the boy and hitting him with sticks, leather belts, belt buckles, and baseball bats. The beatings were ritualistic, involving Mark's being forced to strip naked and lie across a bed. As a result, he was hospitalized three times, but no intervention was ever made. His aunt was instrumental in persuading authorities that the injuries were accidental or the result of fights with other boys.

3. At age eleven, another uncle began to sexually abuse Mark. When he was thirteen, Mark began charging his uncle for sex, which continued until he was sixteen. He also participated in homosexual activity with male peers.

4. Mark began to sniff glue at ten, then progressed to alcohol and every type of drug. By fourteen, he was using heroin and amphetamines intravenously. Also, from the age of ten, he regularly engaged in b&e's, cashed bad checks, shoplifted, and stole cars.

5. Mark has average intelligence but was suspended from school so often that he stopped attending when he was fourteen. He is also very depressed.

Q: *In terms of the abuse, this case features abandonment, foster home abuse, and severe physical abuse involving an uncle. Could you first give a brief assessment of each, and then comment on possible combined effects?*

A: The abandonment obviously happened at a very sensitive and traumatic time for any child. Age five is the onset of the latency period and all of our psychiatric experience tells us that loss of parental figures at this time is a traumatic experience.

This was followed by the abuse at the foster home, and then when it looked like the family could be reconstituted, Mark was subjected to a series of intense abuses in the home. The uncle's physical abuse was particularly brutal and dehumanizing.

If these various abuses are looked at in tandem for some kind of combined impact, one can see that the initial abandonment and foster home abuse set the stage for Mark not being very hopeful in terms of finding relief from powerful, abusive adults in his life in the face of painful situations. And this was subsequently played out when he looked to his aunt when he was hospitalized following his uncle's brutalization of him. At these critical times, his aunt utterly failed to provide any support and protection.

Q: *I take it then that one of the significant effects of the abuses was that each one further reinforced in Mark a world view that people in charge just cannot be relied on. So there are multiple layers of mistrust, cynicism, and gloominess about the world.*

A: And I would particularly emphasize the gloominess.

Q: *I'd like to talk a little about the abuse perpetrated in the foster home. It would seem that Mark at a very early age learned that the outside world was every bit as noncaring and punitive as his own family, wouldn't you agree?*

A: It appears to be remarkable that Mark's aunt and uncle (or the state) selected a foster home that was unable to meet his needs. Even more significant than the physical abuse is that the care givers at the foster home were not attending to his emotional needs, as evidenced by dressing him as a girl. For the latency age boy, such an act is very hostile. Mark must have therefore viewed the world at large as being insensitive to him.

Q: *Mark's parents—the brutalizing uncle and the nonprotective aunt—are common figures in abuse cases involving delinquent youth. However, there are some not so common elements to the physical abuse. I'm thinking of the ritualistic strippings that accompanied the abuse. Aren't sadism and cruelty present here? Also, these are not common elements of physical abuse, are they?*

A: You are correct on both counts. The stripping adds a sexual tone, which confirms our feeling that this father figure is not just angry over some misbehavior by Mark. The ritual aspects and sexual overtones make the descriptive term *sadistic* very appropriate here. I hesitate to use the term *bizarre* because there is not an element of unpredictability.

Q: *The ritualism is not all that common?*

A: Right. I should comment that there is also a sexual component to at least some of this physical abuse. The first example came at the foster home, which was followed by his uncle's sadistic behavior. This causes confusion as to sexual identity and crossing those lines in terms of what we have discussed before—what is nurturance, what is violence, and what is sexual in this world.

Q: *Perhaps you can comment on his selecting glue sniffing at age ten and his intravenous use of heroin and amphetamines at age fourteen.*

A: Glue-sniffing from a psychiatric standpoint is seen as being willing to experience fairly unpleasant effects in order not to feel anything. Glue-sniffing is not regarded as a pleasant high by even the most ardent drug users. It also carries with it the potential to do considerable neurological damage and is a particularly self-destructive, self-negating act. The use of intravenous amphetamines and heroin is remarkable, even more so if the social context happened to be suburban or rural rather than inner city. Again, Mark went to considerable lengths in his attempt to erase his feelings.

Q: *From the time he was eleven, Mark engaged in b&e's, cashing bad checks, and shoplifting. This is suggestive of criminal patterns ingrained at a pretty young age. Are there ties, in your mind, between the abuse and the deeply ingrained nature of his delinquency?*

A: I think that the early onset of the delinquency and the consistency with which it was carried out over the years is very significant. It would be interesting to know more details about his delinquency. Given the onset of the delinquency at age ten and given what was going on in the home, I think that we would certainly assign causative or strongly influential significance to the abuse.

I believe it should be recognized by law enforcement agents and psychiatric personnel that the delinquency pattern can become deeply ingrained starting at a very early age. Thus, we should not dismiss the notion that a ten-year-old can be very antisocial and persistently so.

One other comment is that much of Mark's delinquency was directed toward stealing things. One can easily understand the dynamics with someone such as Mark, unable to find sustenance from people to whom he would turn, garnering things for himself as a nurturance substitute.

Q: *Can you comment, additionally, about the quality of Mark's delinquent acts?*

A: It would certainly be informative to know more about his delinquency as it would help to explain how his delinquency was related to his family experiences. However, we have no specific details regarding the b&e's and other delinquent acts other than an indication that he stole just about anything and everything, probably to get money to buy drugs.

Q: *Could you state the quality questions you believe should be asked about any delinquent acts committed by a youth?*

A: What did he steal? Where did he steal it? How did he steal it? What did he do with the stolen property? And did he steal alone or with others?

The same type of questions can be asked for most kinds of delinquent acts, and can lead to much useful information about the personal make-up of the youth involved.

Q: *At an early age, Mark not only engaged in delinquent conduct with his peers, he also engaged in homosexual activity with them. In your opinion, was this prompted by Mark's confusion over nurturance, violence, and sex?*

A: The potential for Mark to emerge with sexual identity confusion and some homosexual behavior was rooted in even earlier experiences than those of physical and sexual abuse. You'll recall the foster mother dressing him as a girl and Mark's aunt being unprotective. So I think Mark had poor male role models to begin with, one uncle abusing him physically and the other sexually; while he would have seen the feminine role as weak and passive. This immediately suggests to me the prospect of someone such as Mark looking for sexual gratification in a non-heterosexual way. My assumption is that these were the dynamics affecting Mark when he turned to his peers for sexual gratification.

We do need to keep in mind that some homosexual activity in early adolescence is not particularly deviant. However, in Mark's case, the relationships may have been the logical consequence of sexual identity confusions based on his prior experiences at his aunt and uncle's as well as at the foster home. And if you want to look at it this way, Mark's uncle was a homosexual. He chose Mark as a sexual partner.

Q: *It is also interesting to note that Mark did not have a history of violence.*

A: The classic psychiatric interpretation is that depression is anger turned inward on the self. However, in cases such as Mark's, I believe this is simplistic. I think it is surprising that he did not act out in more violent ways, given his history. Instead, he apparently had a great deal of depression. Depression may be a higher level of psychological development than simple, straightforward acting out. From a developmental point of view, it can be argued that it is more appropriate or healthier for Mark to have retained his angry feelings resulting in depression rather than simply lashing out at the world.

Q: *In other words, his intelligence may have led him to the judgment that hurting others was not acceptable.*

A: That's right. And somewhere along the way he may have been able to build in the new mechanisms that we attribute to superego development—namely, guilt—which, coupled with brutalization, can be a powerful combination in the production of depression. You see yourself as victimized, and you have enough sense of what's right and wrong in the world to feel guilt, and the two together pull you into depression rather than allow you to hurt others.

Q: *Given what you have said about Mark's depression being the product of restrained behavior, are delinquent girls, who commonly refrain from more outer-directed delinquent behavior, significantly depressed as a group?*

A: Girls who are subjected to abuse and then to societal pressures that frown on outer displays of aggression would nicely explain why we see so much self-destructive behavior and depression amongst this female group as its members enter adolescence.

Q: *Do you agree that abuse is a lifetime condition that people who have experienced it can manage successfully given the requisite motivation and, perhaps, intelligence?*

A: *Management* is a good term to use, as I do not believe one ever gets over this kind of thing. There are other kinds of psychological trauma that we can think about in much the same sense. For example, children who lose their mother or mother substitutes at an early age never really get over it. Instead, they manage that difficult situation throughout the remainder of their lives, realizing that losses will always be especially difficult for them.

Abuse, of course, is much more damaging because it usually takes place over a more extended period of time and affects one's world view in a more pervasive way. With loss of a parent, other people can step in and make up differences. But with abuse, the damage and scars are really pervasive and not curable in the sense of erasing the experiences.

Q: *As for directly assessing the link between abuse and delinquency in Mark's case, one seemingly could conclude only that the abuse caused the delinquency because the abuse was so pervasive. Remove the abuse and it would seem that no family relationships were left, except for some type of relationship with a passive-dependent mother figure. This does seem to be a case where the two senior males, the two uncles, related to Mark almost exclusively through abusive behavior.*

A: That's right. And in terms of the aunt, she was not only passive but actively colluded with the male abusers to help them avoid punishment or detection. This combination, which we see so often in abusive families, is a deadly one.

Q: *Given the intensity and pervasiveness of the abuse and abandonment in Mark's case, would you expect his antisocial conduct to take a particular course?*

A: We have no particular ability to chart specific behavioral outcomes for victims of certain types of abuse, and I think we need to be careful about this. Having said this, given Mark's ritualistic and cruel physical abuse, it is reasonable to assume that he developed rage feelings and that he would find a way to vent these feelings outwardly in a seemingly sense-less way, or he would turn them inward against himself in a suicidal manner. A third possibility is some type of extreme escape behavior, such as severe substance abuse.

Q: *Will therapeutic intervention be particularly difficult for someone like Mark?*

A: Yes, mainly due to the amount and intensity of his feelings.

Q: *Is it plausible to think in terms of the severe abuse feeding Mark's sub-stance abuse and related criminal activity?*

A: Yes. This is the major dynamic.

Q: *Before concluding, could you summarize the foremost negatives and pos-itives in Laura and Mark's life situations as well as the likely key to their making a positive life adaptation.*

A: As we discussed earlier, Laura is bright and had the experience of one caring adult. Mark, sadly, seems to have had no hopeful life experiences or personal attributes. In terms of foremost negatives, for Laura it is the incest. Ordinarily, sexual abuse of a male child is devastating but in Mark's case, I think that it is the excessive cruelty connected with his physical abuse. His physical abuse was probably devastating in that he could likely make no sense of it.

　　As with all children who grow into successful adulthood, they will need someone who believes in them, will not abuse them, and provide them an opportunity to improve their lives.

Q: *What if their child abuse experiences are not uncovered, inquired about, and addressed therapeutically?*

A: I'm not sure we can predict outcomes, but over and over with our adult patients in great distress, we come to find histories of child abuse that they are disclosing for the first time. Does this mean if they had disclosed in adolescence that all would have gone well in adulthood? I don't know.

Q: *Is traditional one-to-one and group therapy the only road to recovery for the Lauras and Marks of the world?*

A: No. Some victims are able to cope without any therapy, although the experience of sharing the abuse, such as within survivor meetings, seems to be accepted as very valuable.

Q: *What, specifically, about their abuse experiences needs to be addressed?*

A: First, victims need to understand that they are not responsible for the abuse. I can't imagine a good outcome in cases where victims feel that they are at fault. Second, the abuse-victim relationship needs to be labeled as pathological. Otherwise the victim's world-view remains distorted. Third, victims need clarification about what the abuse has done to them. This relates to the confusion over nurturance, violence, and sex that we discussed earlier. It also relates to rage turned against others or self, and to learning that the most terrible feelings in the world can be tolerated without doing something harmful to self or others. Lastly, there are constructive ways for victims to deal with perpetrators so that the force of the emotional aftermath begins to subside.

5
A Researcher's View

James Garbarino

J ames Garbarino, Ph.D., is the author of many books and articles on child development and child abuse. A developmentalist (human development) by training, his research is particularly concerned with the examination of child abuse within family and environmental systems. Formerly on the faculty in the College of Human Development at Pennsylvania State University, he is currently president of Erikson Institute for Advanced Study in Child Development, Chicago, Illinois.

Q: *You have stated elsewhere that the same kinds of environment may be responsible for producing both child abuse and delinquency. Can you elaborate on this, and does it hold true for all types of abuse?*

A: Both child abuse and juvenile delinquency are most likely to arise in high stress/low resources social environments in which the need for emotional validation goes unmet. Thus, the same perverse social environment can, and often does, give rise to multiple problems, including child abuse and delinquency. This is true of physical and psychological maltreatment and, to some degree, sexual abuse.

Moreover, families from which both abuse and aggressive delinquency spring tend to be very negative environments. The fathers of aggressive boys are often hostile to and rejecting of their sons, express little warmth for them, and spend little time interacting with them during the boy's childhood. Parents of delinquent boys have also been shown to be neglectful and lax or punitive, and erratic in discipline. Some studies find the fathers of delinquents to be cruel, neglectful, and often absent, and the mothers cruel, neglectful, and passively helpless. Life with these parents is a far cry from life with the supportive style of child rearing that encourages interpersonal competence and prosocial behavior.

Q: *Many, if not most, adolescents engage in at least minor delinquent acts, and many children experience at least one or two episodes of physical or* *psychologically abusive treatment. Are all these people included within a consideration of the abuse-delinquency connection or are we talking about a much smaller subgroup?*

A: We are speaking of the individuals and families who develop a pattern of abusive and delinquent behavior. This parallels the distinction made by researchers studying runaways, between the "casual" and the "serious" runner.

I think we need to recognize that most children and young people experience occasional incidents of severe physical or psychological discipline or punishment, and we also need to recognize that most youths engage in some sort of delinquent or delinquent-like behavior, but our primary concern is that a chronic, serious pattern of abuse and a chronic, serious pattern of delinquency, particularly aggressive delinquency, go hand in hand.

Q: *Elsewhere you have said that no simple cause-effect relationship is present. Can you explain this?*

A: For example, delinquent behavior can be a cause of abuse as well as an effect. When children and youth engage in delinquent behavior, their parents may respond in abusive ways. We found this in our study of parental and child characteristics that place a family at-risk for adolescent abuse. We found that problematic acting-out behavior can become a stimulus for abuse and neglect when parents are incapable of exerting effective but nonviolent control over their teenage offspring. Several other studies cite this particular cause-effect relationship as a major factor in the abuse of adolescents by their parents.

We must recognize also that abuse can be and often is the result of society's response to delinquent behavior. The clearest example of this comes from situations where delinquent behavior places the child or youth at risk for institutional abuse or abusive victimization by predatory adults (or peers). Investigative journalists and child advocates have documented this connection. Their reports make it clear that when delinquent children and youth are placed in jails, detention centers, or reform schools, they run a serious risk of abuse—physical, emotional, and sexual.

All in all, it seems clear that abuse is linked to juvenile delinquency and delinquency to abuse, though neither is the sole cause of the other. Early abuse can produce a variety of psychological problems and social deficits that set in motion a pattern of behavior that leads to delinquency in later years. Juvenile delinquency can trap the youth in a pattern that leads to further abusive victimization.

Q: *Aren't there cases where a simple cause-effect relationship does exist? For example, when an abused teenager flees the home to escape further abuse and thus becomes a runaway?*

A: Yes.

Q: *If we could prevent the abuse factor, how much could we reduce delinquency and crime rates?*

A: Preventing abuse would be a major step in preventing delinquency and aggressive crime. It would not prevent all delinquency and aggressive crime, to be sure, but each step toward a world free of abuse will be a step toward a world less threatened by delinquency and criminal aggression. Similarly, success in preventing delinquent behavior would reduce the conflict and stress within families and institutions that can escalate into abuse.

Q: *In your prior work, you refer to a vicious cycle of "abuse-delinquency-abuse" and "delinquency-abuse-delinquency." How do these cycles operate?*

A: We know that most of the more serious adult aggressive crimes come out of an escalating pattern of increased delinquency and aggressive acts. The other part of the equation is that often in the initial response to delinquent behavior, whether it is petty thievery, petty aggressive acts, vandalism, and so on, often parents and institutions that deal with youth respond to them in an abusive manner.

Q: *Why and how do some adolescents break out of the cycle of abuse-delinquency-abuse?*

A: What little research we have about this crucial process suggests that the key element is whether or not these youth form enduring supportive relationships with adults and peers who are both nonabusive and nondelinquent.

Q: *Anger seems to be a central ingredient in much abuse and delinquency. What is your understanding of the anger factor, and is anger different for female versus male delinquents?*

A: The experience of being abused produces anger. It produces difficulty in relating to other people. It isolates the young person from his or her peers and from other adults, and those kinds of feelings and social skills tend to lead a kid into an escalating pattern of delinquent behavior.

Anger is the bailiwick of clinicians who seek to understand the dynamics of the abuse/delinquency link. Gender has traditionally shaped the youth's interpretations and response to anger: inward into self-victimization for females; outward into aggression for males. Both suffer from problems with self-esteem down deep.

Q: *You indicate that delinquency can be both a cause of and result of child maltreatment. Does any research indicate what percentage of abused delinquents first experienced the abuse prior to becoming delinquent? Also, is the abuse-delinquency relationship most commonly one in which the abuse experience precedes the delinquency?*

A: There is no research I am aware of that tells us how many abused delinquents first experienced the abuse prior to their delinquency. The best evidence seems to be that mostly it is abuse preceding delinquency, although sorting out the sequences and causal relations involved in maltreatment and delinquency is as complex and difficult as it is vital.

Q: *Does the research show any statistically significant differences of any kind between abused and nonabused delinquents?*

A: Guided by psychodynamic and modeling theories, some investigators have hypothesized that experiencing physical abuse as a child relates not just to general delinquent behavior, but to delinquent behavior that involves violence. Some studies have found that violent delinquents are more likely to have experienced abuse than nonviolent delinquents. One investigator found that 97 percent of the male recidivists ("hard core" delinquents) studied had a history of severe physical punishment and assault in the home. Also, José Alfaro's examination of case records in New York State indicates that abused juvenile delinquents are much more likely to engage in hostile assaults than non-abused delinquents: twenty-four times more likely to commit arson, fifty-eight more times likely to commit rape, and two times more likely to commit physical assault. Overall, data on the relationship between physical abuse and violent delinquency is sparse, but findings indicate that an association may be present.

Q: *To pin this down a bit more, can it be reasonably said that most of the aggressive and violent delinquency is likely committed by youths who have been abused?*

A: Yes, I am sure because without exception, to my knowledge, studies that have examined the life histories of people involved in serious, aggressive crime find the experience of abuse sometimes very early in their lives, certainly in early childhood, and almost invariably in adolescence.

Q: *Does the research say anything about a correlation between delinquency recidivism and abuse?*

A: Not that I am aware of, but my guess is that abused delinquents have a bigger recidivism problem. They are responding to a deep dynamic and thus simple punishment or warning is not likely to deter them, nor is their delinquent behavior likely to be self-limiting. One study found abused children were more likely to resist release from institutions once they were placed there. It's not unreasonable to assume they might be more ready to return to them.

Q: *How do researchers determine that child abuse is, empirically speaking, a significant factor in the lives of delinquents?*

A: Researchers compare delinquency rates for victims and nonvictims. They also compare abuse rates for delinquents and nondelinquents. If victims are shown to have higher rates of delinquency than nonvictims, for example, a significant relationship is said to exist. Retrospective studies of juvenile delinquents consistently have found that these youths experienced maltreatment at rates much higher than the general population. The strength of evidence presented by follow-up (prospective) studies of maltreated children is less clear. Researchers haven't done nearly enough with prospective or longitudinal studies.

Q: *What linkage exists between child abuse and running away?*

A: Frequently a link between maltreatment and delinquency is forged when victims of maltreatment attempt to remedy their situation by retaliating or running away—either choice being considered a delinquent act. While no studies have been found of the proportion of abused children who leave home while still under age, several studies indicate that a large proportion of this country's adolescent runaways have been abused, usually sexually abused, and many left home because of the abuse. I should note that, while many adolescents leave home voluntarily to escape abuse, there is evidence that some "runaway" delinquents are actually "castaways": children put out of their homes by their parents. These victims of extreme child neglect constitute a special class of cases in which maltreatment "causes" delinquency.

What is more, abuse can result when youth run away from home if they fall into the hands of predatory, abusive adults and peers, who may also lead the youth into further delinquent behavior, most notably prostitution, robbery, the drug trade, and other forms of hustling. Studies of young prostitutes reveal that a majority of runaways left home to escape abuse and have experienced significant abuse since becoming prostitutes.

Q: *Does the research suggest that kids who kill their parent(s) uniformly have histories of severe abuse?*

A: Most studies of parricide indicate that most perpetrators are engaged in "reactive" parricide, i.e., in reaction to abuse.

Q: *What, in your opinion, are some important abuse-delinquency research questions which as yet have not been answered?*

A: The most important abuse-delinquency research questions lie in understanding what interrupts the link, and in finding out more prospectively about the very earliest links—e.g., are kids who become delinquent temperamentally inclined to be bad and elicit abuse?.

Also, the possibility that certain stressful family situations or characteristics press toward both maltreatment and delinquent behavior by family members would seem to be fertile ground for research. Many studies have examined the relationship between various family characteristics and child maltreatment, and many others have considered family variables related to delinquency. Little has been done, however, to integrate the two groups.

What is more, the available evidence does not address many historical and cultural issues of great relevance. For example, we do not know whether recent efforts to deinstitutionalize status offenders (and separate them from criminally dependent youths) have strengthened or weakened the link between maltreatment and delinquency. Neither do we know the effects of recent increases in reported abuse (and particularly sexual abuse). Nor do we know if the presumed causal links between maltreatment and delinquency operate differently for different groups within society—more or less powerfully, for instance, for impoverished versus affluent families and communities.

Also unclear is the relevance of these links for intervention. How relevant is a history of maltreatment to therapeutic and correctional intervention in juvenile delinquency? Is it more relevant for some subgroups than others? What are the scientific, administrative, and constitutional implications of accepting a history of victimization as grounds for specifying treatment and/or correctional goals?

Q: *What are the main methodological shortcomings of the existing research?*

A: There is notable inconsistency among the specific behaviors that were measured and labeled as "delinquency" for each study. Some studies examined only violent delinquency, some included property crimes and/or status offenses, and some included various forms of youthful mischief making. Further inhibiting comparisons, some researchers recorded only adjudicated instances of delinquency, others measured reported incidents, and still others, using self-report methods, included incidents unknown to authorities.

The variation among behaviors measured as abuse or maltreatment seems to be nearly as great, although several reports do not include the researchers' operational definition of the term. Different degrees of force are labeled as abusive. Physical, sexual, and emotional abuse are variously grouped or separated, and different types of abuse are at times grouped with some form of neglect. The noncomparability of the key variables in these studies make it unlikely that they can provide a definitive answer to the question of an association between maltreatment and delinquency, although a carefully executed meta-analysis might yield some needed clarification.

Another methodological shortcoming of many of the studies is their lack of appropriate comparison groups. This problem may be particularly troubling for studies assessing the rates of delinquency among maltreated children because rates can be unexpectedly high for various delinquent offenses in different population groups, and thus high rates among maltreated children are not necessarily indicative of an association. Lack of comparison groups is related to another methodological deficiency: absence of inferential statistics assessing the significance of findings.

A problem associated with many of the retrospective studies of delinquents is their use of reports from the juveniles themselves to identify child abuse or neglect in the histories of juvenile offenders. Such reliance on self-report data may result in inflated estimates of abuse. Alfaro's New York study of delinquent and ungovernable children and Lewis' and Shanok's Connecticut study of correctional school and juvenile court wards are notable exceptions.

Q: *Why is it that a subject as intriguing and important as the abuse-delinquency connection does not attract very much research attention? Is it because of the hybrid nature of the subject?*

A: On the one hand, the abuse-delinquency link seems obvious to many people; on the other hand, the prospective research needed is tough and requires long-term commitment. It's hard to motivate people to invest their resources in a difficult and expensive proof of the obvious.

Q: *You presented a number of policy recommendations when you testified before the Senate Subcommittee on Juvenile Justice in 1983. Can you share these?*

A: (1) Increase public and professional awareness of the link between abuse and delinquency, with the theme "most youth in serious trouble are youth who have been hurt." (2) Increase support for research designed to untangle the connection between abuse and delinquency—e.g., what proportion of abused children become juvenile delinquents? What prevents abused children from becoming juvenile delinquents? Do different forms of abuse contribute to different types of delinquency? (3) Assess the experience of abuse as part of the *initial* intervention with delinquent juveniles because it has implications for what kind of intervention is appropriate. (4) Use "experience of abuse" as a criterion for initial diversion out of punitive into rehabilitative intervention programs. (5) Integrate record-keeping among human service agencies so that it is easy to establish the presence of abuse in a youth's case history. (6) Integrate programs targeted at victims of abuse and juveniles diverted into rehabilitative programs so that there is greater efficiency and cost-effectiveness. (7) Support stronger efforts to eliminate institutional abuse in facilities housing delinquent youth. (8) Promote educative programs that teach parents and other adults effective but nonviolent methods of dealing with predelinquent behavior by children and youth. and (9) Increase efforts to protect adolescent abuse victims—particularly runaways—before they are caught up in a pattern of delinquent behavior and relationships.

Q: *Do you have any concluding thoughts on the relationship between child abuse and delinquency?*

A: Child maltreatment and juvenile delinquency are two of the most compelling and perplexing social problems facing the United States in the 1980s. Both meet the criteria proposed by Manis for classification as "serious" problems: They are prevalent, involving millions of people; they are severe, being implicated in many thousands of injuries and deaths as well as widespread emotional anguish; and they are primary, being intertwined with a host of other problems such as poverty, alienation, stress, and economic dysfunction. The evident seriousness of both problems justifies the current high level of public and professional concern.

6
A Judge's View

Hon. William Jones

J udge William Jones is District Court Judge for the twenty-sixth Judicial
District in Charlotte, North Carolina. He is a member of the National
Association of Counsel for Children and of the Board of Trustees of the
National Council of Juvenile and Family Court Judges, and he helped found
Advocates for Children in Court and The Children's Law Center in Charlotte.
He is also past chairman of the North Carolina Guardian Ad Litem Advisory
Committee and is vice-chairman of the North Carolina Supreme Court
Permanent Families Task Force. He has been a featured speaker on the
child abuse–delinquency connection before numerous state and national
organizations.

Q: *How did you first become aware of overlaps between abuse experienced
as a child and later delinquency?*

A: That awareness evolved over a period of time, after I had been hearing
juvenile cases long enough to understand that the labels kids wear into
court are often meaningless. In our system there are abused and neglected
and dependent children and status offenders and delinquents. Not infrequently, kids who come to our attention on a neglect referral for example, could just as easily be placed in another category. In fact, many of
the kids we see in juvenile court could be defined in terms of all those
labels, and the one a particular child receives is more dependent on who
makes the referral and how and to which agency than anything else.
Children who find themselves in juvenile court don't usually have one
discreet, isolated problem, limited to the statutory definition of the offense or status set forth in the petition. Their problems are instead complex and overlapping.

   That reality is compounded by the way services are organized. In my
community, for example, there is a county agency that deals with abused
and neglected children, a mental health agency for the children who need

mental health services, and a state agency that serves the delinquent and status offender population. Unfortunately, as a friend of mine in the mental health field is fond of saying, children and families don't divide up their problems the way we divide up services—and I would add to that, the way we divide up courts.

As these views evolved, I determined to minimize the significance of the labels that are hung on kids and to look instead at the underlying facts and circumstances of their lives and to tailor judicial intervention accordingly. One of the overlaps that became most apparent was the link between being victimized and later acting out.

Q: *When you preside over abuse proceedings involving preadolescent children, is it part of your thinking that they are at risk for later delinquency?*

A: Yes. There are many potential adverse effects and consequences of abuse, and certainly behavioral problems, including delinquent and criminal acts, are high among them. Hopefully, courts and social services agencies are doing a better job now of addressing child abuse and reducing that risk, particularly through our emphasis on keeping families together by resolving the problems that give rise to abuse. Too often in the past we have further aggravated the adverse effects of abuse by dismembering the family.

In delinquency and status offender cases, too, a knee-jerk removal response to misbehavior is, in my opinion, less likely to set a child on a law abiding course than intensive family interventions intended to keep the child at home and to resolve the problems that give rise to misbehavior, including any past or ongoing abuse.

Q: *What is the connection between child abuse and delinquency as you see it?*

A: In simple terms, kids who are abused (at least if the abuse occurs over a period of time, rather than being an isolated incident) will invariably be adversely affected by that abuse. They may have emotional problems or behavioral problems or both, and the severity of those problems will certainly vary from case to case, but invariably there will be problems. Delinquent behavior is one manifestation of those problems.

Q: *You have had involvement with the well-known Willie M. program in North Carolina. Could you briefly explain how this program came about?*

A: The Willie M. Program resulted from a lawsuit that was filed in U.S. District Court in Charlotte, North Carolina. The suit was brought on behalf of Willie M. and the class of kids he and the other named plaintiffs represented, kids who had been in and out of psychiatric facilities, group homes, training schools, foster care, all without significant positive results. It was brought against the state officials responsible for social services, education, mental health services, and training schools. It alleged that the plaintiffs were denied appropriate treatment and education to which they were entitled under various provisions of state and federal law. The class was defined as children under age eighteen who have serious emotional, mental or neurological handicaps accompanied by significant assaultive or violent behavior.

The suit was brought in 1979, and in 1980 it was settled without going to trial. In the settlement the state agreed to establish a treatment program for class members that would provide them with care appropriate to their individual needs for medical, mental health, and educational services. The court order also provided that treatment would be afforded them in their own communities in a continuum of care ranging from residential services through a variety of other out-of-home treatment settings to home-based services.

Over 2,000 class members were identified and in the first year of the program's operation over $22 million was appropriated for their treatment.

The consent order also established a five-member panel of experts charged with responsibility for overseeing the certification process, monitoring compliance with the order and for reporting to the court. The court retained jurisdiction to assure compliance with its order.

Conceptually, it's an excellent program. Implementing it has been difficult in some jurisdictions, but I'm confident that it has made a significant difference for a number of kids who, but for the program, would be in training school or prison.

One of the things that the Willie M. program does most effectively is to be in charge of identifying a child's needs and then, through a case manager, to coordinate the delivery of services to meet those needs— either directly through the program's own personnel and resources, or indirectly from whatever agencies or resources may be available in the community. The program coordinates an otherwise fractured service system.

One of the unique things about the program is that kids can't be refused admission. The certification process is separate so that the local treatment program has no control over whether or not a kid is admitted to the class and therefore to the program. Not only can kids not be denied admission once they are certified, but they can't be excluded from the program. Also, the program can't fail to provide appropriate treatment. It's not an option to say, "This kid is untreatable." What is required is the development of an individualized treatment plan tailored to meet the needs of each child. It's not O.K. to put a child into a slot that happens to be available but doesn't meet his particular needs. If there is nothing in the program, nothing in the continuum of care that meets the needs of a particular child, then those resources have to be created.

Referrals to the program come from many sources—the court, social services, mental health, the schools. It's not just a program for kids with legal problems, and increasingly class members are being identified sooner, before their behaviors are so serious and they are old enough to become involved in the juvenile justice system.

The initial class members all had delinquent records. There had been no treatment resources for them, so they were referred to court. That's no longer true. In fact, one of the benefits of the program, from my perspective as a judge, is that it has diverted many children from the juvenile justice system.

Q: *Do you know what percentage of the more violent clients in the Willie M. program were victims of earlier maltreatment as children?*

A: I don't know the percentage, but from my observation I would say that, in the beginning at least, all of the kids in the program came from grossly dysfunctional families and almost without exception they had been victims of abuse or chronic neglect.

Q: *It sounds like you are persuaded that treatment can be a more viable option for even violent delinquents than incarceration?*

A: Yes, I do believe treatment can work with aggressive delinquents. I would go further and say that if behavioral changes can be accomplished, that will be through treatment, not incarceration. Incarceration punishes the offender and protects society, both legitimate functions, but I don't believe it changes behavior, particularly for these kids. Treatment that works however, is not weekly one-hour psychotherapy sessions in an office, but as the Willie M. program and others have demonstrated, an intensive, comprehensive, coordinated, home- and school- and community-based, hands-on approach that involves not only the child but other significant people in his or her life.

Q: *When you are presiding over delinquency cases, at what point in the proceedings do you give consideration to child abuse as a possible factor in the young defendant's life?*

A: At the dispositional stage, ordinarily.

Q: *Would you allow the defense to submit testimony about abuse during the trial or adjudicatory stage?*

A: Not unless it had some bearing on the offense, where, for example, self-defense is asserted in an assault or homicide trial. Some widely publicized cases have presented that issue.

Q: *Would you forgo a disposition of reform school based on a delinquent having an abuse history?*

A: Not necessarily. The fact that an adjudicated delinquent may have a history of being abused would not exonerate the child, and whether a child is committed to reform school or training school depends on a variety of factors, including prior misconduct, seriousness of the offense, and prospects for treatment or other intervention. Those factors may dictate commitment, regardless of an abuse history.

Q: *Why do you feel that it is necessary for judges in delinquency proceedings to make inquiries about the child abuse factor?*

A: Because that child, in addition to committing some offense, might also be a victim—and if he is, the juvenile court needs to find that out and deal with it if it expects to maximize its opportunity to have a positive impact on that child's life and behavior. If abuse is discovered and is ongoing, then steps must be taken to protect the child from further mistreatment—either by removing the child, or preferably, by intervening in the family to alter that pattern of interaction.

Q: *Does asking a delinquent whether abuse exists in the home present any problems based on invasion of privacy?*

A: No. Whatever right to privacy may exist, I don't think that it includes keeping private the abuse of one's child, particularly when the court has responsibility to craft a disposition tailored to the needs of that child. The question need not be asked in an accusatory way, rather the child should be afforded the opportunity to reveal any such history as may exist. Any legal action that results involving the parents, whether a juvenile proceeding alleging abuse or a criminal proceeding, would of course trigger the rights afforded by statute and the Constitution, such as the right to counsel and the right not to incriminate themselves.

Q: *What other factors do you believe it is important to look for, and how do you rate them in comparison to child abuse in terms of damaging effect on delinquent youth?*

A: It is problematic at best to determine which experiences in anyone's past, whether negative or positive, were most influential in determining that person's behavior. The factors that I see most commonly and that I believe to be the most significant are poor school performance and attendance, substance abuse by the child or parent(s), nonsupport and poverty, and perhaps above all, the quality of interaction between the child and parent(s). A loving, nurturing, involved family can overcome any problem. Certainly the effects of child abuse can be pernicious and I have no doubt that some children become delinquents or status offenders because they come from abusive homes, children who would otherwise not be involved in juvenile court proceedings.

Q: *Is it your experience that delinquents bandy about their abuse experiences as a way of gaining the court's sympathy?*

A: Not at all. Kids are much more likely to be ashamed of that history or embarrassed by it and to therefore conceal it, or to reveal it reluctantly. This is particularly true of sexual abuse. Concern for what might happen to the perpetrator is probably also a factor that inhibits disclosure in some cases.

Q: *How do you, typically, learn that a delinquent has a history of abuse?*

A: From the defense attorney or the juvenile probation officer who accumulates and presents the child's social history at the dispositional hearing. That report should contain information from not only the child and parent(s) but also from school and other agencies and institutions and individuals that have been involved in some significant way with the child or family.

Q: *In the delinquency cases you have seen featuring underlying child abuse, at what age does the abuse usually begin?*

A: Early. Abuse is a complex phenomenon, but it is often associated with an inability to control anger or to express it in an appropriate way and a lack of understanding of normal childhood behavior and development. If a parent has those deficiencies, then abusive treatment is likely to occur at an early stage of the child's life. Later abuse may be triggered by a child's school performance or behavior problems, or substance abuse by the parent. Not infrequently sexual abuse evolves as children reach the midpoint of their childhoods, rather than in the toddler or preschool periods.

Q: *What are the implications of delinquency proceedings in which no attention is paid to the child abuse factor, either out of lack of awareness that the two phenomenon are frequently present in the same child or disregarding the connection on the basis that one's prior victimization is irrelevant to involvement in criminal activity?*

A: An opportunity is lost to minimize the adverse consequences of the abuse history, with the result that the child will continue to be plagued by the problems that have resulted from that abuse. Intervention is less likely to be successful and future delinquency is less likely to be deterred.

Q: *What if few resources exist to serve maltreated delinquents? Is this reason not to make abuse inquiries when processing delinquents?*

A: No. In my mind, one of the highest responsibilities of a juvenile court judge is to be an advocate for needed resources and services. To do that effectively, one must demonstrate the need. Identifying kids who need unavailable treatment and documenting their abuse histories and behavioral problems and the failure of existing resources to ameliorate those problems is one way to demonstrate need.

The Willie M. Program grew out of the frustration of two juvenile court judges who saw some kids over and over again for whom no adequate resource was available and who eventually had to send those kids to training school, knowing that their problems would not be addressed there. They pushed and prodded and complained. They went to the press and, finally, they more or less invited suit. That program exists today in significant part as a result of their advocacy for treatment resources.

Q: *As you travel about speaking to fellow judges and others about the child abuse–delinquency connection, what are the main points you try to get across?*

A: First, that labeling kids in terms of their behaviors or the way they are treated is misleading in that it gets in the way of identifying their needs and providing services to meet those needs. Second, that children and their families are better served by intensive, home-based services designed to help families change to not abusing children and to control the negative behaviors of children, rather than by breaking up the family.

Q: *Would you change any of the legal rules affecting these children?*

A: I don't know that I would change the legal rules, but I sure do think that the service delivery system needs to be more comprehensive and better coordinated in order to make effective interventions in the lives of children and families with multiple problems.

Q: *Courts are always involved after the fact in that there is nothing to adjudicate until a child has been harmed, causes harm, or violates a statute in some other way. Is there anything juvenile courts and judges can do insofar as early intervention and prevention (e.g., of child abuse, delinquency) are concerned?*

A: It's true that there has to be some legally sufficient basis for the court to intervene in the life of a child, but juvenile courts were conceived as a way for the legal system to prevent wayward children from becoming adult offenders. Later, the ever burgeoning volume of abuse and neglect cases was added to the workload of juvenile courts. Unfortunately, for many of the children who become involved in the delinquency system, the die is cast long before the court is in any position to take remedial action, and so, our preventive interventions in those cases may be too late. Abuse and neglect proceedings, to the extent they involve younger children, afford potentially greater opportunities to intervene at a stage when that intervention can make a significant difference for that child and those parents and other children they have. The abuse-delinquency link demonstrates that successful intervention in those cases may well prevent future delinquency.

Outside the courtroom, judges can promote public awareness of abuse and neglect and sensitivity to the issues raised by those cases, including such things as the importance of keeping families together and the abuse-delinquency link.

But having said all that, I want to reemphasize your point that courts do only become involved after the fact. Schools and social services agencies and health care providers and extended family and neighbors and others who have opportunity to identify and report abusive and neglectful situations can intervene at earlier stages.

Perhaps the greatest contribution to preventing abuse and delinquency that courts and judges can make, is to advocate for preventive services, such as school-based sex education programs that would reduce the numbers of children having children, who constitute such a large percentage of the juvenile court caseload; programs that teach prospective parents how to be parents, not just how to change diapers but what children need, how they develop, and what responsible, loving parents do to meet the needs of their children and to nurture and support their development and to cope with the natural frustrations of parenting; quality preschool and day-care services; pre- and postnatal health care services, and so forth. I can't help but believe that public dollars would be well spent on such programs and would, in the long run, reduce costs for training schools and prisons and social services and mental health services and AFDC and medical care and programs like Willie M., not to mention the costs in human terms.

Q: *Historically, delinquents were viewed in rather simplistic terms, usually as bad, wayward, or misguided. More recently, research has revealed that delinquents typically suffer from a variety of individual, family, and socioenvironmental impacts: child abuse, learning disabilities, attention deficits, to name a few. Doesn't this place new and special responsibility on judges, who are charged with making "best interest of the child" dispositions, on lawyers charged with representing delinquents, and on guardians ad litem to whom courts often look for "best interest" recommendations?*

A: Unquestionably, juvenile court practitioners, whether judges or lawyers or volunteer guardians ad litem, must know more than the law to be effective. Child development, the dynamics of sexual abuse, fetal alcohol syndrome, the battered child syndrome, nonorganic failure to thrive, medical and physical evidence of abuse, diagnostic terminology, treatment modalities and availability, child witness issues, learning disabilities, separation and loss, adolescent behavior. The list is endless.

Q: *Do you have any practice pointers for attorneys and guardians ad litem, especially as to the abuse factor in the dispositional stage of delinquency proceedings?*

A: My advice would be never to overlook the possibility of abuse in the background of the children for whom they are advocates. They won't always find it, even if it's there, and if they do uncover a history of abuse, there is still the question of what to do about it. But just being alert to the possibility that abuse, previous abuse, or ongoing abuse for that matter, may be a contributing factor in the behavior of that child—that's the first step in raising our consciousness and understanding of this issue. To be alert to the possibility in literally every such case that the child, in addition to committing some offense, might also be a victim. To do otherwise is to risk missing an important piece of the puzzle and to risk overlooking a critical part of the solution to that child's problems. The other thing that I would say to lawyers and guardians ad litem is that one of their most important functions is to educate the decision maker, the judge; to provide the judge with the information necessary to an intelligent decision in the case of that child; and to hold the judge accountable by insisting on adherence to the rules and by appealing from bad decisions.

Q: *You are known for beginning your presentations on the abuse-delinquency connection by reading selections from* The Adventures of Huckleberry Finn. *We'll reverse things here and ask you to close with one of your favorites, including its significance to you.*

A: I quote selected passages from *Huckleberry Finn* that demonstrate that he was abused and neglected, and that he was a truant and a runaway, and that he was delinquent. Like so many of the kids we see in juvenile court, he could be defined in terms of any of the statutory bases for exercising juvenile court jurisdiction. Huck's father was so neglectful and abusive that the Widow Douglas filed a lawsuit for Huck's custody. ". . . [B]ut it was a new Judge who had just come and he didn't know the ole man; so he said Courts mustn't interfere and separate families if they could help it; said he'd druther not take a child away from his father." That passage is surely the literary origin of permanency planning and the whole notion of keeping families together. Unfortunately, in Huck's case the philosophy was misapplied. He didn't have a lawyer or a guardian ad litem to bring the facts of his mistreatment to the attention of the judge. If he had, Huck might never have made that journey on the river!

7

A Probation Officer's View

Patricia Shannon

Patricia Shannon has been a probation officer for twenty-five years with the Santa Clara County (California) Probation Department. Since 1986, she has served as deputy chief of both the adult and juvenile divisions. Her many responsibilities include management of the Child Abuse Screening Treatment System (CASTS), designed to identify youth referred to the Probation Department for law violations who have previously undetected histories of victimization.

Q: *Could you begin by explaining your department's Child Abuse Screening and Treatment (CASTS) system and how it developed?*

A: In early 1984 the then chief probation officer of the Santa Clara County Probation department initiated a meeting with department staff to discuss developing a program that could determine if there were delinquents with histories of child abuse being referred to the department. The thinking was that probation officers have routinely asked youth about such things as their school attendance, drug and alcohol abuse, but in not asking about child abuse, the department might be overlooking the single most important contributing factor in their delinquency.

Subsequently, an advisory board was created, and the CASTS system became operational within our department in April 1984. Since 1984 CASTS has undergone periodic refinement, and all officers within the department have received training to sensitize them to the possibility of abuse in the backgrounds of delinquents and how to query delinquents about possible abuse. One of the tools we use is a one-page questionnaire designed to guide our officers in obtaining abuse information.

Q: *What are CASTS' objectives?*

A: The purpose is to identify heretofore undetected histories of child abuse among those juvenile who are referred to our department for law violations. There is no question in the minds of department personnel that there is a very strong correlation between a dysfunctional, neglectful, or abusive childhood and acting-out, delinquency behavior. Our main objective is to best evaluate the problems a child may be having that contribute to his or her being in the juvenile justice system as a delinquent referral. We question children about many areas of their life to achieve this objective, with abuse and neglect being one area. CASTS also has a protective objective on behalf of delinquents who are being abused.

Q: *Your department is somewhat unusual in having jurisdiction over delinquents and abused/neglected children. Does this explain why the department has a particular sensitivity to overlaps between delinquency and maltreatment?*

A: Yes, our department is unique in this respect, not only in California but nationally. We continue to be mandated to conduct initial investigations following a complaint of abuse or neglect, although as of a year ago we no longer have ongoing supervision of children found to have been abused or neglected. In virtually all other jurisdictions of the country, the responsibility for investigations following a child abuse report is assumed within social service agencies.

Our Department as well as the local judiciary and police feel quite strongly that the Probation Department should retain its investigatory role in reported abuse cases, mainly on the basis that we view child abuse as a crime and are better equipped to conduct criminal investigations. This has been the hottest debated political issue in Santa Clara County in many years, and the debate is not over.

And yes, because our officers work extensively in the abuse and delinquency sectors, I believe they are especially sensitive to the needs of both groups of children. Most of us have worked here long enough to see significant numbers of children move from dependency or abuse status to delinquency status.

Q: *How are delinquents screened for maltreatment and who asks the questions?*

A: Our procedure is for every youth referred to our department for a status or delinquency offense to be questioned as part of the preliminary investigation by a probation officer in a variety of areas, including the question of whether they have experienced any maltreatment. The question is asked in a sensitive way and in an open-ended manner so as not to lead the child into a false positive answer. The probation officer completes a form reflecting the results of the questioning about maltreatment.

Our officers are trained so that they know how to respond to a youth who discloses abuse. They are also trained to note those occasions when a negative answer does not ring true. In such cases, the officer notes this, and the young person is questioned again at a later time. We also do followup on those minors who disclose, to see to it that they receive appropriate services. Even if the delinquency aspect of a case does not go to the adjudicatory stage or is dismissed for some reason, we still refer the abuse aspect for follow-up.

During 1984–85, we received a grant from the California Office of Criminal Justice Planning to strengthen our service capability to status offenders and delinquents following a CASTS identification of abuse. Although the grant terminated after one year, we have been able to maintain strong followup for adjudicated delinquents who disclosed abuse as part of the CASTS process.

Q: *An argument can be made that asking maltreatment questions is not fruitful because most delinquents either deny being abused or, on the other hand, they may embellish abuse experiences to elicit sympathy from the court. What is your reaction to this?*

A: Anyone who has worked in the field with acting-out youth is aware that they can be manipulative as well as secretive. Because our officers are trained in abuse issues, they have an ability to judge whether a status offender or delinquent is telling the truth about maltreatment. However, the point you raise is well made as our main purpose in raising the maltreatment question is to afford protection and to deal with youth who have been abused in the most appropriate manner. Misstating or withholding the truth makes it difficult to accomplish these objectives.

Q: *What do you do once a delinquent acknowledges a history of abuse? How is this information used?*

A: Once a history of abuse is acknowledged, this information is forwarded to the court and is incorporated as part of the case plan. If the child is found to have committed a serious act of delinquency and is placed in one of our camps or ranches, a special program is set up to deal with the abusive background. If the delinquency is not serious, the child is referred for counseling or whatever community-based resource is deemed most appropriate given the abuse history. If the delinquent is considered still at risk for the abuse and cannot return home, a referral is made to our dependency unit and protective action is taken.

Let me add that when we first started the CASTS program for status offenders and delinquents, there was concern expressed in some quarters that delinquents who had committed serious crimes would not be held accountable, that all the focus would be on their victimization rather than victimizing others. It is evident that the program has not worked that way. Serious offenders are held accountable. However, such offenders, as I mentioned, are accorded therapeutic services to reduce the effects of the abuse.

Q: *Could you elaborate on how you handle cases where you suspect a delinquent has been abused but denies it?*

A: Information gathering at intake is usually a brief process, and consequently, it often takes a while for the officer and the child to develop a strong enough relationship to allow the child to disclose abuse. Therefore, if the officer suspects abuse at intake but the delinquent denies it, the officer notes his or her suspicion on the CASTS form. If the child is subsequently adjudicated a delinquent, the officers at some later point will again ask about possible abuse.

Q: *Upon intake, approximately how many delinquents acknowledge abuse histories?*

A: When CASTS first began, approximately 9 percent acknowledged abuse. However, the percentage is on the increase with 11 percent acknowledging abuse during fiscal year 1986–87. In July 1987 it was 19 percent and in August it was 14 percent.

Q: *Did most of the abuse occur prior to these young people becoming delinquent?*

A: Our experience is that the majority of cases in which a delinquent discloses abuses, the abuse began in early childhood. In some cases, the abuse has continued over the years, but it is difficult to tell whether the abuse was the immediate precipitating event leading to the child's delinquent behavior, such as running away, or parental abuse was in response to the delinquent behavior.

Q: *When you obtain abuse information while doing delinquency intakes, what guidelines do you use in determining whether the case also has to be processed as care and protection? Is it just in cases when the abuse is very recent?*

A: Our prime guideline is whether the child is in immediate danger. Many times, the alleged perpetrator is a stepparent or relative who is no longer in the home, and therefore the child is no longer in jeopardy. If the alleged abuser is still in the home or is in a position to reabuse the child, we refer the case to our dependency unit for further investigation.

Q: *How do you handle a situation when, for example, a fifteen-year-old delinquent girl acknowledges that she was sexually abused by her father until she was thirteen, and there is presently an eleven-year-old sister in the household? Is this sufficient to trigger the child protection part of your mandate to do an investigation concerning the eleven-year-old?*

A: We are very mindful of siblings in the home who might be vulnerable to the same abuse. If we consider them to be at risk, we will refer the case to our Dependency Investigation unit, regardless of whether the delinquent we are dealing with is to return to the home. Such a situation would definitely trigger the child protection part of our mandate.

Q: *The CAST system has been challenged by the ACLU. Can you comment on this?*

A: In 1984 the Santa Clara Valley Chapter of the ACLU contacted our department expressing their view that questioning all delinquents about parental abuse violated constitutional protections of privacy and unwarranted intrusions. They took the position that however abhorrent child abuse is, and notwithstanding that such questioning is proper and necessary in many circumstances, they stated that questioning is only warranted for those for whom there is some reason to believe were abuse victims or whose juvenile offenses bear some relationship to abuse victimization.

   The Santa Clara County legal counsel assessed ALLU's concerns and concluded that questioning all delinquents who come under our jurisdiction would likely withstand a constitutional challenge. We also had several meetings with the ACLU in 1985. However, we have not heard from them since then, so it is not clear to us whether the issue has been resolved.

   The ACLU also expressed opposition to the filing of a child abuse complaint, following a CASTS interview, in the state computer system. The ACLU's concern was that filing names on the basis of a complaint only rendered vulnerable those people for whom no subsequent investigation or determination was ever made. Reporting possible child abuse into the state system is mandated by California's reporting law.

Q: *While on the subject of challenges to CASTS, is asking the question about abuse histories when processing delinquents warranted if you don't have the followup resources to address the abusive condition? Your region may have the resources, but what about probation departments and courts that operate in regions that don't?*

A: It is difficult to imagine regions that don't have any counseling services for abused children. However, where this exists, aggressive action needs to be taken, including use of the media. Asking the question at least affords an opportunity to impose a protective order, if need be, and to ensure the child's basic safety. Santa Clara County and California, in general, have done a great deal of public education about abuse issues.

Q: *Is a formal CAST-type system or intake form with maltreatment questions necessary if a probation department or court is to effectively screen delinquents for abuse?*

A: In my opinion, the greatest accomplishment of a formalized system such as CASTS is to heighten awareness and increase the sensitivity of investigation personnel. The CASTS form is the only way I know to achieve these objectives, as well as record information, in a system as large as our department.

Forms alone will not get the job done. Training staff in awareness and sensitivity is the key—the form is only a tool.

Q: *As for the actual questioning of delinquents about abusive backgrounds, does an intake form help to reduce the chances of individual probation officer phrasing sensitive questions inappropriately?*

A: The form that we use does not address specific questioning or the phrasing of specific inquiries. Instead, our form is general and relies heavily on the trained probation officers asking relevant questions in an appropriate manner.

Q: *Is there anything you would caution probation officers about doing in the screening?*

A: They have to be careful about such things as not asking leading questions, ignoring positive responses, or overreacting to positive responses. They also have to be aware of the manipulations of some youth and not respond to false positives.

Q: *Turning to judicial decision making in these cases, should a delinquent's history of maltreatment make any difference in the adjudicatory phase?*

A: I think we have to be very careful that increased attention to the abuse factor in a delinquent's life does not lead us into the trap of excusing serious misbehavior on the basis of "look what has been done to me in life." However, once a finding of delinquency has been made, our court always takes into consideration a youngster's background, including a history of maltreatment, when making a disposition. Also, a case may change from delinquency to dependency, if appropriate, with an abuse petition being filed.

I cannot comprehend a probation officer or a court not wanting to have all significant background or social history information before him or her at the time of the dispositional hearing.

Q: *Giving attention to maltreatment and other family factors would seem to have no place for juvenile justice reformers who contend that individual responsibility and protection of the community should be the court's primary focus. What is your response to this?*

A: We have a dual responsibility to protect children and to protect the community against serious acting out by children. Dispositional plans must be worked out that address both of these issues. Accepting individual responsibility is one key to curbing recidivist delinquency. Similarly, if we want to reduce future delinquency and criminal conduct, we will have to deal with the various causal factors leading to a child being delinquent. If abuse is a contributory factor in delinquency cases—and we in the Santa Clara Probation Department believe that it often is—we need to address protection *and* therapeutic needs of the child.

Q: *A related question concerns the punishment versus rehabilitation debate that arises whenever extensive inquiry is made about the role of child abuse in delinquency. Are these irreconcilable opposites?*

A: This has been and will continue to be a central debate in the field of criminology. I do not feel that these are irreconcilable opposites. As forenoted, I believe youthful offenders must be held accountable, and the underlying causes of their delinquency addressed. In a related sense, if adult perpetrators of child abuse are not held accountable, their young victims learn a powerful and destructive message. Thus, accountability has to operate at all levels. Punishment that does not deal with causal factors is not a deterrent. Deviant behavior will continue.

Q: *As noted at the outset, your department is unusual in that you have a child protection mandate as well as a delinquency mandate. What about all the probation departments that don't have child protection mandates? Should they, nonetheless, screen delinquents for abuse histories?*

A: Yes, I feel that they definitely should. At the very least, state child abuse reporting laws require all professional persons working with children to report cases of suspected abuse. This responsibility is not removed from probation officers by virtue of another agency, be it welfare or social services, having the mandate to formally investigate such cases. Probation officers are mandated to present a social history to the court when making recommendations to the county when juveniles are adjudicated.

Q: *What about training probation officers? Would you agree that in this day and age all such officers should have training in child abuse?*

A: Absolutely. I cannot comprehend any professional working with youngsters engaged in acting-out behaviors who has not received training in child abuse and neglect. I also cannot comprehend professionals who work with any children, such as teachers, who have not received at least some training.

Q: *You obviously believe that all delinquents should be screened for maltreatment histories. Can you give us a summary explanation?*

A: I will simply reiterate that I strongly believe that a question about maltreatment should be as standardized a question as questions about other aspects of a delinquent's background, family, drug/alcohol use that we have been asking for years. As support for this proposition are the significant numbers of abused children in our country who "graduate" to delinquency, and the high percentage of incarcerated adults who, studies have shown, have high rates of abuse as children.

This is not to say that all abused children will become delinquent or that all delinquents will become criminals. However, the percentages are disproportionately high, and if we are to reduce the number of those people entering the criminal justice system, we will have to take into consideration all family and other factors that have a direct bearing on deviant behavior.

Q: *Would it not be easier for probation departments and courts to forgo searching for underlying histories of abuse among delinquents? After all, such probing can raise thorny problems.*

A: I immediately think of an ostrich, head in the sand. Asking the question about maltreatment does not cause the problem. The problem exists whether or not we ask, whether or not we are aware of its existence. Probation officers and judges have bestowed upon them a great deal of responsibility when it comes time to make a disposition. I, for one, want as much information as I can get before I make a recommendation about a particular child.

Q: *Do you have any final thoughts about the abuse-delinquency connection you'd like to share?*

A: Based on national studies indicating the high percentage of delinquents with abuse history, it is difficult to believe that any significant number of people any longer question the link. What to do with the knowledge that a link exists is probably the central question before us.

The Santa Clara County Probation Department has approached the issues one way, with its CASTS program. Based on our statistics on positive answers, however unscientific the data may be, and on the protective action and case management responses we have been able to make, we have been reinforced in our belief that CASTS is a needed, beneficial undertaking. The program is periodically reviewed, training of officers ongoing, and adjustments made as warranted.

Let me reemphasize that our objective is to obtain all relevant background information on a delinquent child, with CASTS addressing just one, albeit important, aspect of the child's life—possible maltreatment. We have not found CASTS to in any way conflict with our twofold mandate of protecting the community and protecting children within the community. We will continue to hold our delinquents accountable for their misconduct. Hopefully, we will also provide them an opportunity to address painful, unsatisfying parts of their lives so that the chances of future criminality are greatly reduced and they are afforded the opportunity to make satisfactory adjustments in their lives.

8
A Lawyer's View

Andrew Vachss

Attorney Andrew Vachss has advocated for abused and delinquent children for over twenty years. He is a frequent lecturer on abuse, delinquency, and the failure of courts and social services to meet responsibilities to children in their care. He is also the author of numerous articles and books, including *The Life-Style Violent Juvenile: The Secure Treatment Approach* (Lexington Books, 1979), *Flood* (Donald I. Fine, 1985), and *Strega* (Knopf, 1987), the latter two works of fiction covering the same territory. *Blue Belle* (Knopf, 1988), his newest book, will be published this fall. Earlier in his career, he directed programs and institutions for violent youth. His law practice is based in New York City.

Q: *Why have you elected to represent children exclusively in your law practice?*

A: Because I believe in putting my money where my mouth is. Since I repeatedly advocate specialization in this field, I'd be self-contradictory if I were a generalist.

Q: *What is the nature of the relationship between child abuse and delinquency as you see it?*

A: If by *delinquency* you mean crimes committed by juveniles, the relationship between the two is that of cause and effect. This does not mean that all juvenile crime has its genesis in child abuse—it does mean that juvenile delinquents are not biogenetic mutations destined from birth to be criminals. Simply put, delinquency is but one of the predictable outcomes of child abuse. Delinquency may have other causes, and child abuse certainly can have other effects, but the two are inextricably intertwined in many, many cases.

Q: *Are there predictable consequences of being abused as a young child?*

A: Nobody walks away from abuse. Victims act *out*, which is what you would call delinquency, they act *in*, through a variety of self-destructive ways including alcohol and drug abuse, promiscuity, risk taking; or they act "crazy," which is often not an act.

Q: *How much of each type of abuse do you see?*

A: I am unable to separate maltreatment into neat categories. The sexually abused child is almost axiomatically emotionally abused as well. A parent who sexually abuses his own child has certainly, by any rational standard of measurement, also deprived the child of the nurturing, protection, and safety that parenthood is meant to guarantee. The child who is physically abused by one parent is often neglected by the other. Psychological abuse is often misdiagnosed, especially when the victim becomes a predator himself. Maltreatment doesn't operate in a vacuum, and doesn't always express itself with the precise quantification required by the law in formulating, for example, the language of a criminal indictment. A charge such as murder, which must be precisely delineated so as to give notice to the defendant, is often accurate only as to end result, not as to etiology of the events. Body counts are not the same as autopsies.

Q: *What tips you off that one of your delinquent clients has probably been abused?*

A: The behavior that led to the original charges may be a sufficient indicator in and of itself. A ten-year-old child who is sexually attacking smaller children; a series of assaults without apparent economic motive; a shoplifter who obviously wanted to be caught—the list is endless. Parental response is another key element in the diagnosis: Indicators may range from profound disinterest to overt hostility. In fact, there's often a conflict-of-interest problem in being retained by the parents of an accused delinquent if the defense is going to center around the child's own prior history of abuse. Finally, there is the child's own postarrest behavior: The child who speaks glowingly of the detention center tells you something. And the child who attempts suicide tells you something else. The key is to have a high index of suspicion, to always look behind the charges to the motivation for the acts themselves.

Q: *In your law practice, have most of the delinquents you represent been abused?*

A: I don't represent "delinquents." I represent juveniles accused of crime. "Delinquency" is a finding of fact. Not all the children I represent are found to be delinquent (guilty). As to those who are, whether so adjudicated or not—because let's face it, just as the system has a sufficient margin of error so that an innocent child can be convicted, that margin of error can be played the other way and a guilty child can be acquitted— I have yet to see a single chronically violent juvenile with a maltreatment-free past. The trail isn't always easy to follow, especially when working backwards. The emotionally abused child raised to be without empathy who bonds to a street gang and acts in accordance with aberrant values is a classic example. Most investigators would not look past the gang itself when seeking the root causes of the child's behavior.

Q: *Do you ask your clients about abuse experiences or do you look to mental health evaluations or assessments by probation officers?*

A: I do ask my clients about abuse experiences, but I most often learn the *full* truth by an evaluation of their past behavior coupled with their responses. Children don't self-report with great accuracy—their perceptions are not those of the legal system. A client asked, "Were you abused?" may reply negatively and yet fit well within the legal definition of an abused child. I try to use a combination of investigative and intuitive devices, the latter more experience based. And while I often use professional assessments to assist me, I consider probation officers to be adversaries once a delinquency petition or similar accusatory instrument has actually been filed, and I would oppose access to my client at any stage prior to disposition. However, at disposition the probation officer often has a disproportionate influence on the court and should be made a part of the various scenarios defense counsel will offer if at all possible.

Q: *Do most of the abused delinquents you have worked with first experience maltreatment in preadolescence?*

A: Yes. In my experience, abuse that does not begin until adolescence is rare. The most common exception noted is the stepfather/boyfriend, quasi-incest situation. Physical maltreatment rarely begins in adolescence—it tends to be a life pattern, escalating over time.

Q: *In representing accused delinquents with abuse histories, is your main concern presenting this information during the adjudicatory or dispositional stage of the proceedings?*

A: That depends on the legal and evidentiary value of the history. A young child who is now replicating his own sexual abuse by attacking still younger children may benefit from his history being introduced as exculpatory material during the actual trial, while an older child involved with a string of armed robberies may get greater benefit from introducing a history of abuse at the dispositional stage. It's the lawyer's obligation to gather evidence, evaluate it, and then employ it for the benefit of his client. No standardized rules will ever suffice in this regard.

Q: *What other personal (versus legal) information do you believe is essential to have in representing delinquents?*

A: The more you know, the better you are able to protect your client. I would always focus on the kind of information that is most likely to illuminate the behavior with which the child is charged. This can range from an IQ assessment to a psychiatric workup to a family history to biogenetic information (as when you are dealing with incest children), and cover many other areas as well—a language problem, a learning disability, a "suggestible" personality, a hearing impairment—any and all of this and much more can be of inestimable value in a defense. Remember, seeking information is a no risk endeavor. The defense attorney is not a social worker and is under no duty to disclose information not beneficial to his client.

Q: *What is the role of alcohol and drugs in the juvenile cases you handle, particularly in reference to the parents?*

A: I see alcohol and drugs more as an adjunct to larger problems than as a cause. More as symptom than disease. Again, I'm speaking of the chronic offender. I see alcoholism raised as a *defense* in many abuse cases, especially those of sexual abuse.

Q: *Are abused delinquents especially at risk for substance abuse?*

A: Sure. Escape is escape.

Q: *How many of your delinquent clients continue to be maltreated within the home or by one or more of the systems with which they are involved?*

A: Very few of those adjudicated as abused, although it does happen. But the fact that this only rarely occurs is more attributable to careful monitoring than a viable "system." We are engaged in numerous lawsuits concerning children who have been abused out of the home in "placement" of one form or another, and I have represented many children who were badly abused *after* being returned to the home of the supposedly "rehabilitated" parents. Delinquent children are certainly subject to maltreatment while in custody. Predatory gangs still control many juvenile institutions, and in such situations, even "neglect" can be fatal. The lawyer's job isn't over once a client has been sentenced as a delinquent or placed as an abused child.

Q: *How many of your abused clients are also perpetrators of abuse, whether known to the court or not?*

A: I can't separate abuse from crime. Many of my accused-delinquent clients have abuse histories. In fact, I have on numerous occasions represented children originally charged with delinquency who were later placed as abused children once the proof was presented to the court. This is directly age-related: A maltreated infant isn't going to be abusing others, while a teenager maltreated in his or her younger years is quite likely to do so.

Q: *Are there services available specifically for adolescent perpetrators?*

A: Yes, but I locate services on a case-by-case basis depending on the needs of my client. This is all part of the dispositional package. I maintain my own lists, updated on a "What works?" basis. And there are those whose job it is to establish and maintain such registries as well. Some get nice-sized grants to do it, for others it is a labor of love. Access to the lists is what's important to me. The lawyer cannot rely on a child's caseworker or probation officer to put together an appropriate dispositional scenario. The better programs tend to have long waiting lists, so advocacy on behalf of a client isn't confined to the courtroom.

Q: *Among your very young child abuse clients, how many are at risk for later delinquency?*

A: The answer is all of them, depending inversely on the immediacy and intensity of intervention once the abuse is discovered. It almost has a scientific precision about it—the earlier and more effectively we intervene, the greater the prospect of success. But it is my position that all abused children are at risk for continued abuse, for later criminality, for self-destructive behaviors, and for mental illness.

Q: *What, in your view, do these children need in order to avoid the pitfall of later delinquency and subsequent court involvement?*

A: What they need is a sense of commitment by the child protective authorities. The child protective profession has a split personality. It attempts to protect the child and "rehabilitate" the abuser simultaneously. Choices are made along the way, and the pressure to "reunite" the family often supplants the child's individual need for protection. When the state intervenes inappropriately, such as placing the victim of incest outside the home while leaving the perpetrator to be "rehabilitated within the family unit," the child learns that not only will his parents abuse him, but that "society" can acquiesce in that abuse. The victim is punished. A child who believes that no other person shares his pain soon learns to consider only his own feelings. That's how you build a sociopath. And some sociopaths go ambulatory and work on Wall Street, while others go predatory, haunt our back alleys and end up in our prisons and graveyards.

Q: *In your work with violent delinquents, both as an attorney and former program director, do these young people typically experience severe physical abuse or other abuse as children?*

A: Violent juveniles may "choose" to be violent, and they often do. But their ability to make such choices is formed by their early experiences. The prototypical violent juvenile has a history of maltreatment in earlier years, but the connections are not quite as simple to express. The arsonist will most likely have experienced a different form of maltreatment than the mugger. This issue is further complicated by the fact that individuals react to maltreatment individually. Thus, the gifted child subjected to physical brutality may retreat within his mind, sometimes to as far as phenomena such as multiple personality disorders or other dissociative reactions, while the borderline retarded child may robotically imitate his oppressors and emulate their behavior with violence of his own.

Q: *Would you go so far as to say that if they had not been abused they would not have committed violent acts in adolescence?*

A: I'm comfortable with this kind of sweeping statement only as it applies to chronic offenders. An episodic offense may be triggered by a variety of factors unrelated to earlier maltreatment and in no way necessarily indicative of same. Chronicity is much more diagnostic than severity. The predatory, serial rapist tells us far more about his past by his behavior than the youth with no prior record who kills another in a fight.

Q: *Are violent delinquents with abuse histories capable of being rehabilitated?*

A: The very word causes problems. *Rehabilitation* is a medical term, more suited to broken arms than broken souls. For the near-feral, institution-raised child, *habilitation* would be a more appropriate term. Some violent juveniles *can* be given the social, psychological and survival skills to reenter society without significant risk of additional violence. Some cannot. It's an individual assessment and one that cannot be made simply from the facts of the criminal behavior itself. No statute can give you the answer to such a question. Nor will time resolve such problems. As with abuse, the earlier and more competent the intervention, the more effective the result achieved.

Q: *What method(s) do you prefer in trying to reach very aggressive delinquents? For example, there is much rivalry of thought among those who favor the medical/psychotherapeutic model, the educational model, the "shock" model (e.g., the Rahway, New Jersey, State Prison "Scared Straight" program), and the straight "lock 'em up" approach.*

A: Very aggressive juvenile criminals first have to learn the limits of their environment. Much of their aggression is fear-induced, "testing" behavior, and much of it has been learned from prior incarceration. Teaching a young person how to behave in an institution has limited utility. It produces good inmates but lousy citizens. You work with each juvenile as an individual with individual problems and you work not only with what you have been told, but with what you learn everyday—from him and about him. The kid who sticks a gun in someone's face and pistol whips them when they refuse to surrender their money is very different from the kid who commits the same violence after he's pocketed the cash.

As for the Rahway program, I see no value whatsoever in blindly inducing fear. There's a significant difference between *program* and *programming*. Much of the latter could so easily be counterproductive. The old training schools were operated on the idea that they would make the places so horrifying that kids would do anything rather than return. Unfortunately, "doing anything" could range from getting a job to killing a police officer who is in the act of making an arrest. Ask any street cop how he feels about habitual offender laws.

Q: *Do attorneys who represent delinquents have an obligation to try to find out if their young clients have abuse histories? If yes, why?*

A: Any defense attorney has an obligation to search for exculpatory evidence at the trial level, and for mitigating evidence at the dispositional stage. A history of abuse will certainly speak to at least one of those areas, and possibly both.

Q: *Do attorneys need to be well versed in child abuse issues to adequately represent juveniles—whether abuse victims, CHINS, or delinquents? Or is it enough that they have good legal practice skills?*

A: Ask someone accused of SEC fraud if they would be satisfied with a lawyer professing "good legal practice skills." Ask someone who needs brain surgery if he would prefer a G.P. or a specialist. Attorneys don't *need* to be well versed in child abuse issues to represent children; that is, the law doesn't require such expertise as a prerequisite. Yet I find the question to be almost rhetorical, since the added knowledge would increase effectiveness. And if children were *consumers* of legal services instead of recipients, they would insist on specialization and expertise as would any other client.

Q: *How do your child clients view the judicial system? Do they understand the process? What obligation, if any, do attorneys representing children have in this regard?*

A: My clients view the judicial system depending on their capacity to view *any* system. I represent children ranging in age from fetal to what anybody else would call adulthood. Some understand the process, some don't. I think attorneys do have an obligation to involve their clients to the full extent of their client's capacity. But I think we're always going to be working around an analog to the "informed consent" issue. In other words, if a nine-year-old incest victim tells me as her lawyer, "I want to go home because I love what Daddy does to me," I don't think it takes a legal scholar to realize that this is not informed consent and I am not bound to be a mere conduit or mouthpiece for those wishes. This does *not* mean that I utilize a pure "best interests" test in all cases and ignore my client's desires. What it boils down to is this: Treating the client as *participant,* as opposed to *recipient,* is always preferred. It is not always possible. And it's not a balancing test either. It's more that each representation of each child contains both elements—depending on the facts and circumstances, one or the other predominates the mixture.

Q: *What do you feel is the most important obligation an attorney has to a child client, abused or otherwise?*

A: The most important obligation an attorney has to a child client, abused or otherwise, is the most important obligation any attorney has to any client: honest, skillful, effective, committed advocacy. Good representation. I don't think there's any difference between children and adults in that respect, although this opinion may be at great variance with that held by other people.

Q: *What are our law schools doing to train new attorneys to effectively represent children?*

A: Representing children, as I said, is a specialty. If law schools are producing competent and ethical lawyers, they're doing their job. We all know that law schools don't actually "train" lawyers—they provide the knowledge, and experience provides the training. I'm no authority on legal education. It seems to me that specialized work requires specialized training and that the law schools would at least attempt to provide this, hopefully in a multidisciplinary setting with clinical opportunities, if the need were perceived. Until students demand such training, any discussion about its components is premature. If the law schools keep turning out classes that get more excited about investment banking than social change, this perceived need for specialization in juvenile justice is not likely to find its way into the curriculum.

Q: *Why are children such a low priority within law schools and even within the judicial system, where assignment to juvenile or family court is generally viewed as "bottom of the barrel"?*

A: Children are such a low priority within law schools because law students don't evidence a strong desire to make a career out of representing them. The juvenile or family court is often perceived as bottom of the barrel for two reasons: (1) The courts are often closed to the public so the fact that they do the most important work in judicial America is ignored; (2) children don't vote. Court unification is long overdue, especially in a country as status-conscious as ours. It is astounding to me that a judge who routinely makes life and death decisions and tries the most complex and demanding cases in the "Family" Court is paid less and respected less than a judge who does nothing but decide *ex parte* motions in a "Superior" Court. The irony of "promoting" the most experienced Family Court judges to a "higher" court may be lost on the public, but it is not lost on the litigants.

Q: *Is it your opinion that the abuse factor of a delinquent's life has to be addressed if recidivist behavior is to be reduced or made less intensive?*

A: *Recidivism* is another word for *chronicity,* the difference being that the recidivist is defined by his arrest for additional crimes—this same unit of measurement is not applied to the chronic offender who has not been caught. Chronicity is more diagnostic, in my opinion, than any other factor. If the underlying cause is not treated, the effect will continue to repeat itself. Once calcification has set in, once the offender is psychiatrically committed to a course of conduct, the notion of rehabilitation has no foundation in reality.

Q: *Is the fact that a delinquent has been abused as a child justification for his or her delinquent conduct?*

A: Explanation is not justification. If a past history of abuse satisfied the legal requirements of a "justification" defense, the prison population would be substantially depleted, and society would be in a state of siege. The buck has to stop somewhere, and accountability is a significant component of functional, as opposed to philosophical, rehabilitation. Nothing "justifies" evil acts. If maltreatment is a cause, rehabilitative treatment will be effective in direct relation to how early it is applied. But even for those for whom we "risk" such treatment, we may still have to employ incapacitation during the course of treatment.

There's another side to the "justification" coin, one that desperately needs to be confronted and addressed. Criminal behavior is essentially a matter of *choice*. And child abuse itself is criminal behavior. Those who postulate that child abuse axiomatically produces more child abusers are guilty of defaming and degrading those who have overcome this incredible handicap. The essence of the battle against recidivism is that behavior is *self*-controllable. Child abusers are *inadequate* parents who simply don't know how to act within minimally acceptable standards. Such individuals benefit significantly from the standard rehabilitative interventions. Or they are *mentally ill* and benefit in direct proportion to our therapeutic ability to address their specific disorder. Or they are *evil*.—nothing less than predatory criminals who produce their own victims. And such individuals should access whatever rehabilitative opportunities as may exist for them while inside a penal institution. If the fact that a juvenile was abused as a child is "justification" for criminal conduct, so is a previous history of child abuse "justification" for the child abuser.

Q: *The ITA/ABA standards and the Model Juvenile Delinquency Act recently developed by the Rose Institute in conjunction with the American Legislative Exchange Council both reject a rehabilitative approach to delinquency, instead favoring individual accountability and protection of the community. What are your views on a rehabilitative versus a punitive approach to delinquents?*

A: I wrote an entire book on this subject, and I'm certainly not satisfied I fully addressed this complex and emotionally loaded issue even then. In short form, punishment as conceptualized by a "justice" system is futile when applied for its own sake. Such "punishment" is too remote in time from the offense and too unrelated to the reality of the offense to "teach" the offender—or even to deter him. For punishment to be an effective tool, it has to be a reasonably foreseeable consequence of unacceptable conduct and has to be directly and proportionately related to that conduct. The child who is locked up as punishment and finds himself in an environment that exalts "might makes right" may well "learn" from the experience. But society will not benefit from what he has learned. Incapacitation, on the other hand, has a separate and distinct function—it protects society while treatment is taking place. That the length of incapacitation may be made proportionate to the severity of the underlying offense does not per se render it punishment in my eyes, although I acknowledge that it may be so perceived by the offender. I think the "there's no such thing as a bad boy" advocates actually created monsters, who came to believe the rhetoric of the juvenile courts and woke up to reality while doing a life sentence.

Children are not adults, and they deserve different treatment. We agree that children have a special quality that we call *juvenileness* and that implies a state of immaturity and the ability to intervene before the seed comes to full flower. Children are not adults, but for those who have committed dangerous acts, this different treatment may well take place in a closed setting. Accountability and rehabilitation are not, in my mind, antithetical terms. Whatever one's individual belief in rehabilitation of a specific offender, we must look at that individual offender's dangerousness in making any treatment decision. No predatory beast should be free to walk among us, regardless of the etiology of his behavior. And how we respond to such a person during his incapacitation, whether we focus on treatment or deterrence, will always be an individualized decision.

Q: *What do you say to professional people, judges included, who caution against uniform screening of delinquency cases for underlying child abuse unless there are resources available to address the abuse?*

A: The lack of resources is a societal disgrace. The presence of an abuse history may well be a defense, no less valid than a defense such as insanity. Would you eliminate the insanity defense on the ground that we don't have enough institutions to treat the criminally insane? If we fail to break the cycle of early abuse and later criminality, we perpetuate it. So if we don't develop the resources, we're not serious about fighting crime. Saying we should not screen delinquency cases for a prior history of abuse because we don't have enough resources to address any abuse we find is not a solution to a problem: It is a capitulation to everything that is wrong in our society and an abdication of fundamental responsibility.

Q: *What needs to be done to upgrade judicial management of children's cases and legal representation of children?*

A: Open the courts to the public and you will see a substantial improvement in judicial management. I understand that there are potential drawbacks to this, although they apply, in my opinion, far more to delinquency proceedings than to those involving abuse and neglect. Full "public" access may never be possible, and perhaps should not be. But the process should be observed and reported. The names aren't important, but the games certainly are. Provide a secondary appellate process for juveniles and you'll see a radical upgrade in the effectiveness of representation; that is, provide a process by which there is an independent review of abuse, neglect, and delinquency cases other than by the lawyer who originally represented the kid. Where there is no scrutiny, there's little reward for competence and little penalty for below-standard performance.

Q: *Can the delinquency battle be won at the backend of the intervention system through increasing the effectiveness of our responses to delinquents, or must we primarily concentrate on assisting abuse victims and/ or prevention?*

A: The delinquency battle cannot be won at the back end. The best program in the world will still be dealing only with the hard-core precipitate. I don't believe child abuse can truly be "prevented" in most cases, but I do believe that juvenile crime can be—by early, intensive, skillful, and committed intervention.

Every dollar invested in a professional child protective continuum of care is the equivalent of thousands of dollars invested in juvenile justice. And of hundreds of thousands invested in criminal justice at the adult end. In fact, the systems should long since have been merged into a consortium treating the "whole" child. The child protective system should not surrender responsibility when a formerly abused or neglected child is charged with delinquency. And the juvenile justice professionals should focus their "prevention" efforts on child protective work. We know how monsters are made, but government seems to lack the will to interfere in the process while there's still time to do so.

Q: *Any final thoughts about the abuse-delinquency connection, especially in regard to attorneys and other practitioners in the field with child clients?*

A: I think the fact that you and I and others in our profession take this connection as already established just isn't enough. I don't think that we'll even be at the plateau from which we should start to climb toward effectiveness until the abuse-delinquency connection is burned into the mind of the judiciary and becomes part and parcel of the way that every defense attorney looks at a case involving a child. Whether you're representing an abused child or a "delinquent" child, whether you're representing today's victim or tomorrow's predator, you are *defending* that child.

The public has some quantum of sympathy and empathy (although less than I would like to see) for the abused child, and none for the violent delinquent. Unless and until they can see the connection between early abuse and later violence so that their own self-interest is activated, and unless and until that self-interest impacts upon politicians, legislators, and the judiciary, for attorneys who defend kids to recognize the abuse-delinquency connection will not be enough. True defense of children is nothing less than defense of this country and all we believe in as a people. It requires that the abuse-delinquency connection, which has a moral, ethical, scientific and legal foundation, be preached until it becomes the law, the rule, and the heart of the land.

9
One Additional View

José Alfaro

J osé Alfaro is director of training and research at the Children's Aid Society in New York City. Previously he was coordinator of the Mayor's
Task Force on Child Abuse and Neglect in New York City; and director
of the New York State Assembly Select Committee on Child Abuse. In this
latter capacity, he conducted the most comprehensive study ever done on the
relationship between child abuse and delinquency.

Q: *Could you briefly describe your study?*

A: The study was conducted between 1973 and 1978 and was an attempt
to measure systematically the connection between abuse and delinquency, with two large samples of children.

The first sample consisted of children who were reported to child
protective agencies or the children's courts (now known as family courts)
in eight New York State Counties during the early 1950s. It totaled 5,136
children. These children and their siblings were traced forward in time to
see how many had later contacts with the children's court for delinquency, or PINS offenses.

The second sample consisted of 1,963 children who came before the
family court in 1971 and 1972 for either a PINS or delinquency offense.
These youths were traced backwards to determine how many had had
prior contact with the family court or child protection agencies as abused
or neglected children.

Q: *What are some of the study's major findings?*

A: We found that as many as 50 percent of the families reported for child
abuse and neglect had at least one child who was later taken to court as
delinquent or PINS. In one county, the rate of delinquency and status
offenses among the children in the study was five times greater than
among the general population. We also found that 21 percent of the boys

and 29 percent of the girls reported as delinquent or ungovernable in the early 1970s had been reported as abused or neglected at some earlier stage in their lives. As high as these percentages are, they are conservative based on incomplete data due to missing records in some counties. No doubt, if we had had all the agency or court contacts, these figures would have been higher.

Q: *Where did the impetus for the study come from?*

A: The New York State Assembly Select Committee on Child Abuse held a series of hearings throughout the state as a prelude to making statutory changes governing the child protection system. Many professionals commented on the large number of abused and neglected children who return to the courts in their teen years as delinquents or PINS. Several Family Court judges were especially emphatic about this. The testimony resulted in the State Division of Criminal Justice Services funding the study I directed as a means of empirically clarifying the abuse-delinquency relationship.

Q: *Is the relationship between child abuse and delinquency primarily causal or something else?*

A: It may or may not be. What seems more important is that our study showed that a significant percentage of abused and neglected children have later involvement with the court as delinquents or PINS. Given the high percentage, we should be providing abused and neglected children a broad range of services to reduce the likelihood of later court involvement. An important finding of our study was that such a range of services was not available. This remains pretty much the case today. As early as the 1970s, the National Center on Child Abuse and Neglect made a number of treatment recommendations that included assessments, mental health programs, and compensatory services such as Head Start and therapeutic daycare for children. These are services that exist and can help to counter the adverse effects of abuse. Unfortunately, abused or neglected children too often receive none of these services or perhaps one or two at most.

Q: *Did you find any connection between physical abuse experienced as a child and later, violent delinquency?*

A: We found that those delinquents in our second sample who had been abused or neglected previously were more likely to have committed violent offenses than those who had not been maltreated. There is a tendency to think that abuse has more harmful long-range consequences than neglect but our study did not show a significant difference when we examined the violent offenses.

Q: *Is there insufficient emphasis on neglect in the child protection field and among the general public?*

A: Approximately 85 percent of all reported cases in New York are for neglect. I suspect that this holds true for most states. Nationally, 55 percent of the child fatalities are due to neglect rather than abuse. In New York City, the most recent study on fatalities indicated an even higher percentage, over 60 percent. So yes, I think that neglect is underemphasized.

Q: *Were there any consistent patterns whereby specific types of abuse linked to later, specific types of delinquency?*

A: Not specifically in a narrow one-to-one sense. However, as I mentioned earlier, there was a relationship between earlier maltreatment, including neglect, and later violent offenses as committed by the delinquents in our second sample. Thus, the maltreated delinquent seemed to us to be different than the nonmaltreated delinquent.

Q: *Were other problems common in the families you studied?*

A: The families in both samples were rather different than other families in the communities where they lived. They tended to be larger, had a greater percentage of illegitimate children, and had more one-parent households. Also, a significant number of the families were dysfunctional, and some had contacts with the courts and social service agencies going as far back as the 1920s. They were truly multigenerational problem families.

Q: *In terms of adverse impact on the children involved, how did the abuse factor compare with these other family problems?*

A: It's a good question, but our study did not address this.

Q: *Is there any question in your mind that young child abuse victims are at risk for later delinquency, and that the abuse element of delinquents' lives needs to be addressed to reduce their at-risk status for recidivism and later criminality in adulthood?*

A: There is no doubt in my mind, and yes, we definitely have to address not just the abuse but also the neglect aspect of delinquents' lives. Neglect is perhaps even more crucial to address because it is generally more pervasive than abuse. Chronically neglected children are extremely difficult to reach. Neglected children may be more damaged because they are unloved and unwanted. Abused children may often be wanted and loved, although in a pathological way.

Q: *What in your opinion is the most significant implication of the child abuse–delinquency relationship?*

A: It is the need to recognize the potential treatment needs of the young children we know have been abused or neglected, and to do something about it. The greatest failure, the biggest gap, is the national failure to meet, adequately, the needs of preadolescent children who have been identified as abused or neglected. The future requires us to commit the resources to meet these children's needs over a period of years.

Q: *Why doesn't the reality of violence and more and more people being incarcerated in prisons motivate society to address more closely causative factors such as child maltreatment?*

A: I'm not sure how much the average citizen understands these connections, despite our efforts to explain them. Also, there may be confusion over whom we should be focusing on: the adult criminal, the violent juvenile, or the young abused or neglected child. We're not saying, "Let's coddle the criminal"; we're saying, "Let's cuddle the child."

Q: *Do you believe that most serious crime and delinquency would be ended if we could prevent child abuse, as some people have suggested?*

A: Yes, I think this or at least a significant reduction would be the outcome. However, there are some big "ifs" involved. The real question is whether we, as a society, have the will to try. Confronting us is the challenge to break the intergenerational cycle of violence. To do so, we need to focus on the very young children—the next generation of violent people unless something is done. What fits here is the notion most parents have of wanting their children to be better off than they are. Another part of this is the increased role of schools in addressing health care issues. I would, also, put new emphasis on teaching students how to care properly for a child.

Q: *You have written: "Understanding the possible relationship between child abuse or neglect and juvenile delinquency or ungovernability could*

*have enormous significance for the way our society approaches the prob-
lems of child maltreatment and juvenile misbehavior." What did you
mean by this?*

A: We tend to see abuse and neglect only in terms of stopping it. We don't
have a future perspective. We don't see a central part of the child protection role as reducing the effects of abuse and neglect. We need systematic
followup, periodic assessments every two to three years, and a variety of
services over a long period of time. One important rationale for doing
this is based on the persuasive data we have about maltreated children
being greatly at risk for later delinquency. Another basis is the body of
research, however unsophisticated, indicating a high number of adult
criminals with histories of maltreatment.

  The causation issue is less important than the fact of early identification in the child protective system of thousands of children who later
will be processed through the juvenile justice system. Not to adopt a
long-term approach is to miss an important opportunity to help these
children develop normally and avoid later delinquency and criminality.
The social costs of this failure are great.

Q: *You have also said that legal distinctions between different categories of
children and families are often "misleading and hinder treatment efforts."
Can you explain this?*

A: We get hung up pinning a label on a child, and the label a particular child
gets is often the product of who sees a child in distress and when. If it
occurs early, the label tends to be *abused* or *neglected*, somewhat later
it's *PINS*, and eventually it's *delinquent*. These are all labels we use at
different points, all to describe what is frequently the same child. In looking at the narrow categorical problem, we tend to not see the other di-
mensions of the child's life, now and into the future. Despite all the talk
about holistic approaches, our response system generally looks at only a
single, specific problem area as if it has no connection with other problems which are present. It's an artificial construct. Often, the funding of
categorical programs forces this overly narrow approach.

  I'm reminded of a cartoon I saw a few years ago of an old lady
visiting a doctor who tells her he is going to send her to doctor number
2 for one problem, doctor number 3 for another problem, and so forth.
In the last panel of the cartoon, she looks up at the doctor, plaintively,
and asks: "Doctor, isn't there someone who can take care of all of me?"
Similarly, maltreated children need to be served by a single, multiservice
agency that deals with the whole child and his or her family.

Q: *You have called for an overhaul of the entire system of categorical programs. What specifically needs to be done?*

A: I think that we have to look anew at systems we have developed to help children and families. It's hard because for so long we have utilized the categorical or individual problem approach. I don't have the answer to how, exactly, services would be organized, but I am convinced that we have to force ourselves to see services delivered to these children and their families in new ways. I'm confident that if we can do this, we have the intelligence and ingenuity to do the rest.

Henry Kissinger used to talk about the need for a "conceptual breakthrough" in foreign policy as an essential first step on which change could be built. This is what's needed in the delivery of services to children and families.

Q: *Is this holistic approach being used anywhere?*

A: I don't think so, at least not in the United States. In Scotland, a children's hearing is used that avoids labels such as *abused, neglected, CHINS,* and *delinquent.* Instead, the focus is on the child's underlying needs rather than on acting-out behavior.

Aspects of the Scottish hearing can be seen in juvenile mediation services such as those provided by the Children's Aid Society and other agencies. This may be the beginning of reconceptualizing how we approach children and families in trouble. However, I am not sure whether mediation is the result of a perceived need for improved service delivery or because the juvenile case load is so great the judges are unable to try all the cases.

Q: *To what extent are delinquency courts aware of the frequency with which delinquents have abuse histories and earlier involvement with the child protection system?*

A: I do not think it is systematically known, as an issue. I hope there is a greater sensitivity to the abuse-delinquency connection today, and that courts will explore it as part of their evaluations of delinquents. Courts can check their own records to see if a delinquency case has previously been before the court for abuse or neglect. However, since only about 20 percent of all abuse and neglect cases go to court, even conscientious cross-checking within the courts will only uncover a small number of connected cases. There is no easy way for courts to cross-reference cases with child protective agencies. A lot of information stored in one system never gets to the other.

Certainly, children with abuse or neglect histories will have some different treatment needs, and it's important to know whether they have been maltreated. I just don't think it is very feasible for courts to gain open and continuous access to child protective service records, and therefore the information will usually have to be obtained some other way.

Q: *Is it essential for delinquency court judges to be aware of the maltreatment factor? If yes, why?*

A: I think so. I think that Judge Dembitz and Judge Follett and others were saying this in 1973 when they testified before the New York Select Committee. The reason, again, is that in order to fashion meaningful dispositions, judges have to know the nature of a juvenile's basic problems. New York's dispositional structure is tied to what is in the "best interest" of the child and the child's needs. These questions can't be answered just by referencing the delinquent act. Judges have to know why a particular child is a particular way. Any abuse or neglect would be one important piece of information.

Q: *How might delinquency courts coordinate better with the child protection system as well as with other systems (e.g., mental health, education) that may have valuable information about a juvenile awaiting disposition of the court?*

A: The person who prepares a dispositional report for the court should have the authority to obtain relevant information about the child from all other systems involved in the child's life. To make full use of this data, I believe that the person preparing the report should be trained in a mental health related field or in social work. Using someone with the proper credentials to assemble this information would encourage other agencies or systems to be more willing to share whatever information they have about a child.

Q: *Are confidentiality laws a barrier?*

A: We always use the sacred dogma of confidentiality in tough cases. However, when a child and his family are known to three or four systems, I am not sure what the confidentiality is. Professionals involved with these cases are not interested in publishing sensitive information in newspapers or misusing privileged information. I don't think that hiding information or being afraid to talk to someone furthers the common objective of helping children in trouble.

Q: *Are you persuaded that abused children, including those who have become delinquent, have the capacity to change?*

A: I think so. I think that it is generally accepted that people can make changes although not uniformly in all situations. One study I am familiar with assessed young abused and neglected children who did not subsequently become delinquents. The single most important explanation for this seemed to be that these children formed a significant, positive relationship with an adult at an early age. This is the "significant other" theory, a person—whether a relative, teacher, coach—who provides positive direction and emotional connection for the child.

Q: *How do you reconcile holding delinquents responsible for their behavior, on the one hand, with directing services at a delinquent's underlying condition, including a possible history of child abuse?*

A: Society has a legitimate interest in sending out a clear message to rule breakers that there will be consequences. It's a didactic function of the law. This is different from understanding why someone is breaking the law. Understanding why a person can't or won't change their behavior tells us what we have to do to get them to change. For some personalities, such as psychopaths, about the only thing we can do is lock them up. Dr. Menninger tells us that other personalities commit crimes so that they can be punished. For these people, punishment may become an emotional reward for criminal conduct. There is not a single explanation for why people break laws; human beings are too diverse.

So we have to make a clear distinction between making and enforcing rules and what we are going to do to see that people don't continue to break rules. The latter calls for understanding each individual—which should not be confused with condoning. The ultimate goal is to have fewer people who disobey the rules of society, which are intended to prevent one person from hurting another.

Q: *Can you elaborate on the issue of punishment?*

A: That's a difficult question because in seeking to hurt someone who has hurt another, we run the risk of all of us becoming like the assaulter. It's a bind, and I don't have a clear answer. Punishment is sometimes nothing more than revenge, getting even. This is an emotion that does not appeal to me. On the other hand, I want some assurance that someone who has assaulted me will not do it again, and I will fight back.

From a pragmatic point of view, we want to do whatever is most effective in preventing someone from reoffending. Psychologists indicate that punishment is the most effective way of achieving this with some personality types, but not all. For some people, we don't know what to do because of our limited knowledge base, so we simply incarcerate as a means of protecting society. As a citizen, I don't particularly like having to pay $50,000 or more to incarcerate someone for a single year. This motivates me to search for something more cost effective.

What it finally comes down to, for me, is that we have to commit our resources to very young children as soon as they are identified as abused or neglected. If we wait for them to become acting-out delinquents, I'm afraid in many cases it is too late. We simply don't know enough to effect change in some, perhaps many, of them. I am uncomfortable writing off another human being, but given our level of knowledge and limited resources, we don't have much of a choice. Not all delinquents are too far gone, but some have been too damaged.

Q: *So you are not too hopeful about intervention with delinquents?*

A: I see the delinquency end of things as a last, least opportunity more than anything else.

Q: *What about the present court system, which deals with children in trouble, whether maltreated or delinquent? Is it adequate for the task or do we need a new approach?*

A: As I mentioned earlier, I think we do need new models such as the Scottish hearing system, where issues are addressed that sometimes are overlooked or ignored in the adversarial system.

Q: *Elsewhere in this book, several people have strongly recommended that delinquency courts should screen all incoming delinquents for child maltreatment histories. Do you agree with this?*

A: Yes. It gives the court a more complete sense of who the child is, what he has been through, and why he is acting the way he is. I think this is important not so much for the adjudication but for the disposition.

Q: *What else would you like delinquency courts to do that presently is not common practice?*

A: Judges and others who are close to these cases have to do a better job of explaining to the public the connections between maltreatment and delinquency. Our society is very sympathetic to young abuse victims but not so sympathetic to adolescent victims. Our ratio of sympathy declines as the child gets older, especially when acting out begins. With preadolescent victims, we fault the parents. With abused CHINS and delinquents, we fault the child. I don't think this is helpful, especially when we know that one-third of the abuse and neglect cases, nationally, involve adolescents; next to children under two years old, adolescents have the highest abuse mortality rate.

Q: *Aren't some people inclined to think that abused adolescents get what they deserve, that they provoked or instigated their own abuse?*

A: Yes, and we also say that it's not really a problem because adolescents can protect themselves. I think this is a dangerous approach because we then see children killing their parents. If the child protection system is unresponsive to adolescents, it may contribute to these young people's misunderstanding of what they should do to protect themselves. This is what happened in the Jahnke case several years ago.

Think about it from the child's point of view. What must a young person think? He has been abused for years and nobody pays much attention until he begins to act-out, and then he gets defined as the problem. He or she must wonder, "Where the hell have you been all my life?"

Q: *You, for one, don't believe that most legislators buy the "pay now or pay later" approach. Yet isn't it true that many maltreated children, especially those for whom no meaningful intervention is provided, wind up being very costly to society? How do you sell the economics of earlier and more effective intervention?*

A: I don't think that we as a society have a clear sense of the total cost of delinquency and crime. Unfortunately, we don't have any studies that would show the percentage of adult crime that is directly related to offenders who, at an earlier point in time, were part of the child protective system as abused or neglected children. However, I think we would find that it is cheaper to invest at the child protection end than at the criminal justice end where the cost of incarceration can run $50,000 a year or more per person.

So having a comprehensive economic profile would certainly be helpful in getting society to invest more strongly in child protective services, although the economic argument alone does not carry the day. There are competing priorities in our society, and citizens have to decide what they want and need the most.

Q: *In considering the abuse-delinquency connection, your main point is that we have to make a much greater investment at the abuse end when children are first identified as maltreated. How can this policy be effected?*

A: Perhaps through a combination of creating greater awareness about the connection and the economic argument. A central problem is that our governmental system and our society, overall, are very short-term in outlook. It's a societal defect.

Q: *What about a child development approach, getting more people to understand the basics of child development and how destructive maltreatment is to normal or healthy development?*

A: I am a little more hopeful about this approach. Something seems to be going on in our society that speaks to a growing concern about child welfare. We can see this in recently increased legal rights for children, the campaigns against the use of corporal punishment, and child protection laws.

All of these suggest a growing appreciation for the child as a person. How widespread this appreciation is, however, unclear. Still before us is learning to care as much for someone else's child as our own. All of this pertains to a national attitude about children that is coming to understand that children really are our future, the future of humanity.

Q: *What is the current status of the national child protection system?*

A: Presently, it is in chaos due to insufficient resources. We have not clearly articulated what we want the system to do. We also may have overpromised what the system can do. When a child, under the supervision or care of child protective services, is badly hurt or even killed, there is a tendency to view the tragedy as symptomatic of a failed system. In such cases, child protective services receive a great deal of criticism, and it is hard for many people to put into perspective the task child protective services have been given with minimal resources to accomplish the task. The child protection system needs to do a better job of explaining to the public the complexity of many cases.

Q: *How do you feel about narrowing statutory criteria for state intervention in abuse or neglect cases, which some people are calling for?*

A: I see a difference between narrowing and clarifying. A lot of state child protection laws are very general, even vague about what constitutes the conditions warranting state intervention. These need to be clarified, including specific conditions that constitute abuse and neglect, and defined degrees of harm or threatened harm.

It is generally known that abuse and neglect laws are frequently invoked as a means of getting services for families. A person should not have to be labeled abusive or neglectful to obtain needed services. However, I do not favor narrowing child protection laws until there is an alternative means of providing services to children and families in need of them.

Q: *Do you have any other thoughts about our present child protection system (CPS)?*

A: I heard a presentation not long ago by a Connecticut psychologist who was studying the impact of child fatalities on CPS workers. The researcher had previously studied Vietnam veterans and the tendency of the American public to blame them for the war. He analogized to CPS workers and the tendency we seem to have to blame them for abuse and neglect. There is something about being closely associated with a confounding problem that creates a taint. It's a perception that we have not examined closely enough in our own hearts.

I'm not suggesting that CPS agencies do not make errors, but in other human service professions we grant a considerable margin of error. Yet when a child known to a CPS agency is killed, there is a tendency to want to crucify the agency. There is little sympathy for the extremely difficult task the rest of us have given CPS.

Moreover, we have no performance standards for CPS agencies and workers, who in this regard are almost alone in the human service field. We cannot tell how well they have performed at the time a case is finished. Success seems to mean no major incident three to four years after closing a case. In fact, we know very little about CPS decision-making processes, the factors and forces that shape it correctly or incorrectly.

As for the so-called child abuse backlash, some people have been treated badly by CPS and understandably are angry. However, I think we need to keep in mind that other people do not feel victimized. In a training session several weeks ago, one of my agency's staff told how he was questioned by school officials who noted bruises on his daughter. At first, he felt angry. Then he realized that other people really cared about his child. He felt glad about that.

Q: *In closing, can you provide state and federal policy makers with a short list of the most important things to be done in response to what we now know to be a significant relationship between child abuse and delinquency?*

A: First, let's stop being dumb about it. We have enough data to know that a very important relationship exists between maltreatment and delinquency. Second, we have to develop a more effective early intervention strategy that helps young victims minimize the effects of maltreatment and other injurious experiences. We can begin with the children who have already been identified, by doing such things as reducing child protection worker case loads and allocating resources to treat young children. Then we can do a better job of identifying more children who are being maltreated. If we want real delinquency prevention, here is the place to start.

10
Closing Argument

David N. Sandberg

As noted in Chapter 1, thirty professionals from various disciplines and parts of the country gathered at the Johnson Foundation's famous Wingspread in Racine, Wisconsin, in April 1984 to more closely examine the relationship between child abuse and delinquency. Jim Garbarino served as moderator and task master.

After dinner our last evening together, Jim asked if I would share with the group any feelings I had on the subject. By this time, we had invested two days in intellectual exploration. He granted me license to speak without regard for empirical considerations, to speak whatever I felt as one additional way of getting at the multifaceted abuse-delinquency connection.

I shared two feelings. The first was my conviction that the relationship between child abuse and delinquency was the most important development in the juvenile justice field in the past ten years—since the heyday of Senator Birch Bayh and the onset of deinstitutionalization in the mid-1970s.

At the time, this sounded like an overstatement even to me. Today, it strikes me as an understatement. In fact, I am convinced that if we could prevent child abuse, we would eliminate much crime and delinquency, not to mention an assortment of other societal ills and personal afflictions encountered in adolescence and adulthood. This is not to suggest that all or most victims of child abuse grow up to be destructive members of society. However, based on mounting research evidence, it is increasingly clear that a disproportionate number of highly destructive and self-destructive members of adult society share a common experience of severe maltreatment as a child.

The other feeling I expressed in Racine concerned the shocking human condition of a large number of delinquents. It is not just the beatings, kickings, and sexual assaults they have suffered. It is mothers and fathers calling their own children *shithead, whore, scum,* and worse; mothers and fathers violating normal boundaries and reasonable codes of conduct; mothers and fathers leaving their children to fend for themselves at the age of three or four and even younger. It is also the learning disabilities, attention deficit disorders, poor dental hygiene, serious physical injuries and illnesses never properly attended to, self-mutilations, school failure, suspensions, and finally, expulsions. Almost always, there is alcoholism and drug addiction by parent and child. Worst of all are these young people's mounting feelings of despair, frustration, and rage.

Amid all of this human tragedy—and the deplorable condition of this class of children in the United States is a tragedy—I submit that there is hope. More than this, the child abuse–delinquency connection offers an extraordinary opportunity to move beyond crisis management and burnout, which are as much the result of a lack of ultimate purpose within the child protection and juvenile justice systems as a lack of resources.

A threshold question in a world of limited resources is whether to concentrate at the front end of the problem when children are first identified as maltreated or the backend once a youth has been found to be delinquent. Without question, we need to target both adolescent delinquents and preadolescent abused and neglected children, keeping in mind that the former are often the latter partially grown up. Having said this, I will also say, as Andrew Vachss and José Alfaro have before me, that if we are to win the war, it must be at the front end doing major intervention with young children as soon as they are identified as abused or neglected.

Some will argue that even this is too late, that the war can only be won by carrying out primary prevention campaigns. In an ultimate sense, they are probably right. However, we have before us hundreds of thousands of known abused and neglected children. They are the immediate concern. If we can do well by them, we will see major downline gains in terms of reduced delinquency and crime.

How, then, should we proceed?

If we are looking for an experience that offers young victims a potential offset to the harmful effects of maltreatment and the likelihood of later delinquency, none is more promising than a successful educational experience. The research is clear: Recidivist delinquents uniformly do not succeed in school. Put another way, youth who do well in school seldom wind up in delinquency court. In my own law practice, I cannot recall more than one or two of my delinquent clients graduating from high school. On the contrary, school has primarily been a bad experience for them almost from the day they first arrived in school as five- and six-year-olds, notwithstanding the dedicated efforts of some individual teachers, usually at the elementary level.

Therefore, it is exciting to think that if we can provide a meaningful educational experience for abused and neglected children, we will go a long way in reducing the risk for later delinquency. The key lies with insisting that all children have a meaningful educational experience and addressing all major impediments, including child abuse and neglect, to children having such an experience.

The great promise here is that parents and intervenors are more apt to agree on educational success as an ultimate goal than any other intervention rationale. At a broader policy level, it is essential that we do everything in our power to keep these children in school, to prevent them from being forced out, being thrown out, or dropping out.

Another critical variable in the lives of abused and neglected children is alcohol and drugs. Although all children are at risk for substance abuse, maltreated children are especially vulnerable because (1) their parents often are substance abusers, (2) outcast children usually join a peer group of similar children who invariably use alcohol and drugs, and (3) alcohol and drugs can deaden emotional pain, of which the young people we are talking about often have a great deal.

For these children, the odds are great that alcohol and drugs will one day control their lives. When this time comes, just as when the time comes when they leave school prematurely, the incidence of their delinquency will rise and intervention attempts will be far more difficult.

A third critical variable is society making a long-term commitment to these children. If we are serious about prevention of future ills, cases should not be closed until there is an affirmative finding as to four issues: (1) The child has come to terms with his or her maltreatment experience; (2) the child has demonstrated academic success at age-appropriate grade levels; (3) the child is not at risk for future abuse; and (4) the family has addressed any substance abuse issues.

At the other end of the child abuse–delinquency spectrum are hundreds of thousands of delinquent youth and the juvenile court system charged with managing them. This system is presently under attack as critics renew the charge that the great rehabilitation experiment of the twentieth century has been a failure.

In truth, the experiment is still in its infancy. For one thing, the child abuse element of many delinquents' lives is just now being understood as a key remedial factor. For another, services have seldom been available to meet the multiple problems so characteristic of many delinquents. Judge Jones talks about the Willie M. program in North Carolina, perhaps the only all-out effort in the United States to reach hardcore, recidivist delinquents before they plague society for years to come.

Notwithstanding this, some critics would replace rehabilitation with the *just deserts* approach, which emphasizes offender accountability and protection of the community, neither of which is incompatible with rehabilitation. The problem with just deserts is that it ultimately offers no hope because it does not address causative factors such as child abuse and associated feelings of rage. Moreover, a singular strategy of punishment will not work with a class of youth who have been punished for as long as they can remember.

This is not to suggest that truly violent and dangerous youth should not be punished or incarcerated. In cases involving especially serious crimes against people (such as murder, attempted murder, rape), recourse should ordinarily be had to state certification laws whereby minors above a certain age may be tried within the criminal justice system. In this manner, there is not misuse of the juvenile justice system which, otherwise, is a highly appropriate system for our nation's delinquents.

Where incarceration is called for—either within juvenile reform schools or adult jails or prisons—holding facilities need to be humane. There also need to be parallel remediation efforts on a scale similar to the Willie M. program. Such efforts will fail more often than they succeed, yet it is clear beyond question that we cannot afford not to make these efforts. At some point, we need to make human contact with these alienated, angry people and they with us. Otherwise, we can predict continuing patterns of victimization and perpetration.

Other critics of the juvenile court system have promoted the *rights* model. This is based on the perception that the system has historically provided too little treatment and benevolence and therefore a juvenile's greatest protection are his legal rights. In fact, many juveniles were and some continue to be treated very badly by the state. The worst cases feature status offenders who are incarcerated and then abused by state workers.

"Rights" proponents have achieved significant gains for young clients, including a series of United States Supreme court cases in the 1960s. The best known is *In re Gault*, in which the Court held that the United States Constitution guarantees a delinquent the right to an attorney.

The problem with a narrow "rights" approach is that legal rights ultimately do not mean very much unless they include a right to treatment or meaningful rehabilitative services for those who are found delinquent by the court. Andrew Vachss is correct when he says that a lawyer's job in representing young people after a finding of delinquency is just as important as during the pretrial and trial phases. This is in marked contrast to representation of adult offenders.

Other critics do not advocate any particular model or philosophy. Instead, they are cynical about positive outcomes—with some justification— and accept the *maturation* or "aging out" theory, which is based on an analysis of national crime data and the age of offenders. This theory holds that offending youth evolve out of their violent ways by the time they reach their mid- or late 20s. As the theory goes, they do so regardless of the type of intervention strategies or sanctions imposed on them in their adolescent and young adult years.

Unlike the just deserts and rights approaches to delinquents, there is nothing positive about the maturation approach, which is really not an approach at all. First, the fact that an individual ceases to appear as a crime statistic is hardly a comprehensive statement about that person's life and his or her impact on society. So I have to ask, "What do they evolve into?" The answer in many cases is continuing substance abuse, and abuse or neglect of their own children. Is society truly to take comfort in this? Second, are we really to stand by during the especially destructive adolescent and early adult years, yielding to the inevitability of maturation, which in all likelihood is really a simple shifting of mayhem from the streets to the home?

Most troublesome about the maturation theory is the implied assumption that recidivist delinquents are too disturbed or too entrenched in patterns of antisocial conduct to be rehabilitated or habilitated. I do not quarrel with the proposition that some may be too damaged to redirect their lives. The problem is that we cannot tell for sure which ones can succeed. If we were to select candidates for hopelessness, surely Sterling Winslow would have made the list. Therefore, we have no choice but to commit to this class of youth as a whole.

Moreover, because we rarely provide abused delinquents with the full range of services they need, we have no way of knowing the potential of therapeutic and other interventions. In the years to come, perhaps the Willie M. program will help tell us.

In building a stronger juvenile court system for delinquents, we might consider that the rehabilitation, just deserts, and rights models all have important contributions to make and that setting up these strategies as irreconcilable opposites and devoting great amounts of time debating their relative merits does not get us very far. Regardless of the approach taken, the task at hand is and will continue to be enabling young offenders to come to terms with forces within themselves that, if unresponded to, will lead to crime and dysfunction in adulthood.

Foremost, abused delinquents need to be assisted in understanding their maltreatment and defusing its life-threatening components. Sterling Winslow put it this way: "In order to make changes within myself, I had to deal with the abuse and the rage. These things affected everything I did and said." In this respect, he probably is illustrative of countless delinquents with abuse histories, although one can only guess how many receive the opportunity he did to understand and control their abuse.

We would also do well to remind ourselves that abused delinquents are at far greater risk for serious difficulty in adulthood than abused adolescents who are not delinquent. In addition to their ongoing patterns of criminal conduct, abused delinquents are typically deprived of schooling as a mitigating experience, and they are involved in alcohol and drug use at unusually high rates.

At some point, it must be asked whether we have the will to forge new child protection and juvenile delinquency policies based on the child abuse–delinquency connection. It is disturbing to hear José Alfaro say that nothing ever came out of his 1970s study, notwithstanding considerable initial legislative interest.

Amid all the competing needs and priorities in American society, however, I think we do have the will. As imperfect as they are, our child protection and juvenile justice systems represent an important commitment to children's well-being. At an individual level, the work of Sterling Winslow, Pam Hagan, Rowen Hochstedler, Jim Garbarino, Judge Jones, Pat Shannon, Andrew Vachss, José Alfaro—and many others—has contributed to the abuse-delinquency connection's being increasingly recognized as having major implications for the youth involved as well as for American society.

We are also witnessing the early development of far-reaching policy analysis with the child abuse–delinquency connection at its core, the most outstanding example being Judge Friedlander's landmark essay entitled "Child Maltreatment and Delinquency: Making the Case for Preventative Criminal Justice" (see appendix D). A continuum of destruction from early childhood maltreatment and deprivation to delinquency and crime can now be seen. Just as clear are the answers to these largest of all societal problems: early childhood intervention and societal commitment to ameliorative child development opportunities.

As we head into the last decade of the twentieth century and toward the twenty-first, there is ample reason to believe that the child abuse–delinquency connection will occupy a central role in forging new responses to delinquency, in helping to rejuvenate the juvenile justice system, and in reframing the national crime prevention agenda. It is now abundantly clear that delinquency attaches itself to child abuse so frequently and so intensely that we can no longer afford to process delinquents without asking about child abuse histories and providing remedial opportunities to address the abuse. Granted, most delinquents will need more than this to alter the course of their lives, but coming to terms with child abuse experiences is the foundation on which other gains are predicated.

The implications of the child abuse–delinquency connection for preadolescent abuse victims and those who work in the child protection field are no less significant. Simply put, we must make major service investments on behalf of young victims. No longer can we allow abused children to slip away, knowing all the while that many will resurface at a later time—less innocent, less malleable, less cooperative.

We must do these things, foremost, because we adults owe a duty of care to all young people and especially to those who are disadvantaged by reason of having been abused.

We must also do these things because society as a whole stands to gain immeasurably from our having done so.

Appendix A
Excerpts from the NCCAN Final Report, "The Role of Child Abuse in Delinquency and Juvenile Court Decision-making"

Empirical Findings

- 66% of the 150 Odyssey House residents had child abuse histories, almost all involving a parent perpetrator.
- 61% of the boys and 75% of the girls had been abused.
- physical abuse was by far the most common type of abuse (53 of 99 boys, 32 of 51 girls). 27 of the 85 physically abused residents had been subjected to physical abuse by more than one parent.
- the next most common abuse was sexual (4 of 99 boys, 19 of 51 girls), with 3 of these 23 children having been sexually abused by more than one parent.
- 10 of the 99 boys and 4 of 51 girls had been neglected, and 8 of 99 boys and 4 of 51 girls had been emotionally abused.
- overall, 36% (54) of the 150 youth experienced multiple abuse, meaning the same abuse at the hands of more than one parent and/or two or more different types of abuse.
- the mean age of onset of abuse was 7 years old, with only 10% of the 98 abused youth experiencing abuse commencing in the teen years.
- the average *severity of abuse* score index for physical abuse was 2.4, indicating that on the average the physically abused children in the study were very seriously assaulted; and the mean *frequency of abuse* index score was 5.7 years.
- only a small number of the 98 abused members had been identified as abused prior to entering treatment following involvement with delinquency courts.

Grant No. 90CA901/01,
National Center on Child Abuse and Neglect
(1982–83).

- families of abused members were typically multi-problem families, e.g., almost half of the abused children had parents who were violent to one another, double the rate for families of non-abused children.

- of the 150 youth, the girls experienced significantly more "other than abuse traumas" (2.4 avg.) than the boys (1.7 avg.).

- 83% of the 150 had engaged in 3 or more different types of illegal activity, with theft, burglary and assault being the most common offenses.

Significant Factors Other Than Abuse/Neglect

Adoption

In five of the 150 cases, adoption appeared to be a critical factor in the child's participation in delinquent conduct. Interestingly, the adoptive families were relatively problem-free compared to most of the other families, yet the subjects themselves carried a sense of being unworthy, "not part of." In two of the cases, the acting-out behavior commenced at the same time the subjects learned that they were adopted rather than biological offspring. None of the five were abused. In numerous other cases, adoption was present but did not appear to be as critical a factor as in these five cases.

Significant Deaths

In five cases, the subjects (all males) experienced loss of the father figure through premature death during the subjects' pre-adolescent period, and this factor appeared to be key in understanding the later delinquency. In addition, two boys also lost mothers at the same time and another lost an older brother six weeks prior to the father's death. As with the adoptive cases, the families involved were otherwise relatively problem-free and none of the four were abused. However, it is apparent that the surviving parent in three cases faced major pressures as a direct result of the spouse's death. In the other two cases, the boys subsequently lived in a series of foster home placements.

Psychological "Death" of a Parent

In many cases involving members of both the abused and non-abused groups, divorce or its functional equivalent meant more than a mother and father no longer living together. Far more significant in 40 cases was the complete disappearance of the non-custodial parent, usually the father. Most subjects commented that they never saw this parent again after the split and did not know his/her whereabouts. A few indicated that a period of years went by without having any contact with the non-custodial parent.

"Black Sheep" Syndrome

In several cases, the child was never able to fit into an otherwise reasonably well-functioning family. One case was classified as emotional abuse due to the college-educated parents continued degrading of the subject and comparing him unfavorably to his six success-oriented siblings. In the other cases, it was not clear why the subjects were "black sheep," yet the records clearly illustrate that these children had not bonded with their parents as their siblings had.

Severe Parental Psychiatric Disturbance

In 36 cases involving parents of both abused and non-abused members, the records revealed severe psychopathology on the part of one or both parents based on suicide attempts, hospitalization for nervous breakdowns, and/or family history of serious disturbance. Such families were usually multi-problem families, with the psychiatric disturbance linking to other factors such as alcoholism, divorce and, in some cases, abuse. Eight subjects reported a parent being hospitalized at least once due to having a nervous breakdown. It is to be noted that a far greater number of parents had serious psychiatric disturbance if one uses as a bases their alcoholism and/or abusive, sometimes bizarre and sadistic, treatment of their children. However, only parents meeting one of the above-noted criteria was included here.

Parental Suicide

Although 14 of the residents reported that a parent had attempted suicide, only one parent was successful. At the time of the incident, the male subject was two and he did not learn until age 13 that his father had first shot the boy's mother and her father, both of whom survived, and then killed himself. The mother, who never remarried and overprotected her son, reported that the boy's delinquent conduct coincided with his learning the truth about his father.

Early Childhood Medical/Psychiatric Problems and Failure of Parent to Respond Appropriately

In one case, the male subject appeared to have an inherited psychiatric disturbance and presented serious emotional and behavioral problems from birth. In another case, a male subject was born five weeks prematurely, accidentally ingested kerosene at one, experienced a severe concussion at 1½, and cervical ademitis and possible athetoid cerebral palsy at three. This latter case was carried by Odyssey House as neglect, but has in common with the former case which was not carried as an abuse/neglect situation, parental inability to respond to a child's obvious medical and psychiatric problems. As the child's needs intensified and continued to be unmet, the boy with the psychiatric disturbance attempted to hang himself at age 12. The following year his mother divorced the father, remarried, and moved a far distance away. In the neglect case, the parents divorced when the boy was 10. Since then, she has lived with a series of boyfriends and has continued to be non-responsive to her son's special condition. In a third case, the male subject was described by the Odyssey House psychiatrist as "a chronically institutional-ized, impulse-ridden young man (age 15) who has carried the diagnosis of affective disorder." Both the boy's parents and their parents have histories of serious psychiatric disturbance, thus preventing them from responding ap-propriately to this boy's disturbance.

Parental Sociopathy

A deeply ingrained anti-social life style on the part of parents was noted in six cases. In five of the cases, abuse and/or neglect were also present, and all of the families were noted as "bad"—all family members involved in crime and violence. One subject had two older brothers serving time for manslaugh-ter, another's father was imprisoned for raping the boy's older sister, a third father was a major drug dealer. The fourth father served ten years in prison, a fifth father was incarcerated for rape, and a sixth father did seven years for armed robbery. Not surprisingly, the six male subjects had more extensive (and violent) delinquency records than most of the other subjects. Four of the six subjects also reported chronic alcohol and/or drug use by one or both parents.

Large Family

Although only one of the 150 NCCAN subjects was a single child and the great percentage came from homes with three or more children, in only one case did the large family dynamic seem to play a major role in the subject's alienation and subsequent delinquency. This was not a "black sheep" case as Odyssey therapists noted that there were no normal bonds involving any of the eight children and their parents. However, a note was also made that this child, in particular, felt "emotionally crowded out," i.e., the family was too big and the parents too lacking in nurturing ability to reach all the offspring in some minimal way.

Hyperactivity

Hyperactivity or "attention deficit disorder" was noted in 12 cases, involving six abused and six non-abused subjects. All were self-reported. In most of the cases, it was not known when the onset of hyperactivity occurred. Consequently, it is not known whether the hyperactivity resulted from the abuse or stimulated it. Quite likely, far more subjects were hyperactive in pre-adolescence but were not included in records forwarded to Odyssey House by parents and school personnel.

"Smother Mother"

In three cases involving non-abused males, the mother responded to the father's death (one by suicide, another from illness) or divorce by overprotecting the child. These families had a small number of siblings. The critical loss had occurred in the pre-adolescent period, and the subjects' subsequent acting-out appears to be a dramatic attempt to break away from the mother's infantalizing them.

Underage Parent

An apparently central factor in one case was a male subject's mother being 14 at the time of his birth. The mother left the boy with a babysitter when he was four, and he did not see her again until he was 13. In the interim, he was raised by his father. The absence of a maternal bond, central to this boy's poor development, is closely linked to the underaged mother who subsequently abandoned him.

Retardation

Given that Odyssey House does not ordinarily treat a retarded population, it is not surprising that only one of the 150 subjects was retarded. However, nine others tested in the low normal range, with IQ scores in the high 70s and low 80s. Six of the nine were also abused children as was the mentally retarded subject.

Superior Intelligence

Eight subjects tested at 120 or above and were clearly of a superior intelligence. Five of the eight did not report any abuse and in these cases the parents quite clearly did not perceive the child's special condition. It is likely that the IQ factor was a significant element in the weak parent-child bond, further exacerbated by the parents' inability to understand "differentness." Whether the high IQ factor in the other three cases somehow prompted the abuse is unknown.

Stranger Abuse

In one case, a male subject was forced to engage in oral and anal intercourse at age seven by a male stranger who picked the boy up while hitch-hiking. The family is otherwise somewhat unique among the 150 NCCAN families in that both parents are high school graduates, have only two children, and indicate no divorce, substance abuse or psychiatric disturbance. Yet, the child has been engaged in extensive delinquency (assault, vandalism, arson, theft) since age nine. The boy is filled with rage, and the rape at age seven stands out as the one major negative factor in his life. Coupled with this may be the parents' inability to recognize the severity of the molestation trauma and the boy's need for much care and attention immediately following the event.

No Parental Limit Setting

The previously-noted sociopathic families illustrate one kind of failure to set limits for children. Some of these children were abused and also were "disciplined" for getting caught committing a crime, not because it was wrong but because they got caught. In contrast, the 150 case histories uncovered only one family which overindulged the child, set no limits, and always came to his rescue when in difficulty. Not surprisingly, the Odyssey records note this 16-year-old as "arrogant" and "self-centered."

Institutional Malfeasance

In one case, a subject experienced 15 foster home placements since the age of three when his parents' rights were terminated due to physical abuse and neglect. Not surprisingly, he is filled with rage and has exhibited very threatening behavior.

Other Observations

1. Delinquent behavior began for many of the subjects at about age 11, although non-delinquent "acting-out" behavior frequently began earlier. Often a divorce seemed to occur about the time a child was 10 or 11.

2. Very few of the abuse cases involved parents trying to "pound sense into" an adolescent following some disruptive behavior by the child. Where this did occur, it was part of a continuing chain of abuse going back prior to adolescence.

3. As commented on above, members of the abused group often had a complicating condition such as hyperactivity, borderline retardation or physical ailment of which the parent(s) had no understanding and which seemed to prompt the parental abusive treatment.

4. Over and over, members of the abused and non-abused group reported very negative school experiences.

5. Members of the abused group rarely mentioned a sibling who might also have been abused. The autobiographies are strangely silent about this as they are about much of the writers' own abuse.

6. In response to the question "Which parent loves you the most?", a standard question all Odyssey House residents are asked to answer when writing their autobiography, members of the abused and non-abused group almost invariably responded that both parents loved them but perhaps mom (or dad) a little more. It was not uncommon for some of the abused subjects to answer, "Both my parents love me but I'd say my mother more because she does not hit me." Rarely did abused subjects state that they were not loved although one abused girl stated "My family is not a family, it's a war." Only where the perpetrator was a step-parent, often no longer living with the biological parent, did the abused subjects vent anger at the perpetrator or indicate this parent did not love them.

7. The parents of both subject groups, but especially the abused group, were very caught-up in their own problems, e.g., low income, drinking, divorce, psychiatric disturbance. The parents seemingly did not have the time, energy or wherewithal to deal with their children's problems.

8. Seldom did any of the 150 subjects mention a positive role model in their lives, other than a frequent reference to a favorite grandparent, now deceased and seemingly made into the all-loving parent these children never had.

9. The most common parental prototypes in the 150 families was a bullying father figure, often alcoholic, and a passive-dependent mother experiencing nervous breakdowns. Also, these fathers seemingly became especially hostile as their daughters entered puberty, likely related to highly threatening sexual feelings toward the daughter.

10. Over and over there was a picture of a child finding only tension, chaos and/or abuse at home, often accompanied by feelings of rejection. This, in turn, likely led the child to a search for family outside the home via joining a negative peer group.

Appendix B
Testimony Submitted to the U.S. Senate Subcommittee on Juvenile Justice on "The Relationship between Child Abuse and Delinquency"

David N. Sandberg
Director, Program on Law and Child Maltreatment
Boston University School of Law

I am pleased to have been asked to provide testimony on the very important issue of child abuse and its relationship to delinquent behavior.

Before sharing some thoughts with you, I would like to briefly state who I am so that you understand my frame of reference. From 1970–1977 I was Director of Odyssey House Inc. (N.H.), a private residential treatment program for court-referred delinquents. In the early 1970s, not much was known about child abuse and I now know that many residents passed through our system without their abuse ever being uncovered. But by the mid-1970s, the therapeutic world as well as the general public began to learn about child abuse and as we learned we began to pay more attention to abusive parental behavior.

Consequently, in the last years of my tenure as head of Odyssey House in New Hampshire, my staff and I came to understand that the paramount therapeutic task we often faced was not remediation of drug abuse or delinquency but child abuse. In addition to working to keep my program alive financially, I also served as an individual and group therapist for delinquent youth, many with histories of abuse.

In the following years, I obtained a law degree and began to involve myself in abuse issues from a legal perspective. This has involved representing juveniles in abuse/neglect proceedings and in custody disputes where child abuse emerges with regularity. I am also a research attorney at Boston University School of Law, and for the past year I have been principal investigator for a research project on "The Role of Child Abuse in Delinquency and Juvenile Court Decision-Making," funded by the National Center on Child Abuse and Neglect (HHS).

This project has afforded me the opportunity to review prior research on abuse-delinquency and to think systematically about my experiences with juveniles since 1970. We are only just now beginning to put together all the research, but I can share some general findings.

First, 66% of 150 delinquents referred to Odyssey House from 1974–1982 by New Hampshire courts were found to be abused or neglected. We defined "delinquency" as any act committed by a minor which if committed by an adult would be a criminal offense. The most common delinquent act among our sample was breaking-and-entering. "Child abuse" consisted of physical abuse, sexual abuse, emotional abuse and neglect. We do not have a breakdown as yet, but I am comfortable saying that the great majority of cases involved physical and/or sexual abuse.

I wish to emphasize that 66% is a conservative figure. We did not make a recording of abuse, for example, where a child was hit on the buttocks with a strap beginning at age 11 or 12 as "punishment." Others might consider this abuse and they may be correct. I make the point simply to underscore the conservative nature of the findings. In addition, we did not record neglect or emotional abuse except where it was severe or co-existed with physical or sexual abuse.

Concerning reliability of the data, the 150 delinquents in the sample had to meet a threshold requirement of having lived at Odyssey House for at least 30 days and for whom there was at least one quarterly psychiatric review in their medical chart. Typically, resident statements about abuse or neglect were made within therapy sessions and subsequently followed-up on by therapists and recorded in the charts. Consequently, we believe that our data is at least as reliable as that obtained by researchers in a single interview or question-naire session with unknown delinquents. No control group was used because our purpose was limited to identifying abuse among a delinquent population only.

The 66% abused/neglected delinquents were typically between ages 5–12 when the maltreatment occurred; the maltreatment was pervasive in na-ture and extended over a period of years; and the parental figures were most often a brutalizing biological or step-father and a passive non-intervening mother. These families were usually of a lower socio-economic nature and featured multiple family "negatives" in addition to the abuse, including pa-rental alcoholism and spousal violence.

Another aspect of the research included an assessment of any patterns linking specific abuse experiences with later, specific delinquency. Although the data has not yet been analyzed, I believe I can safely make two observa-tions about this. One, teen prostitution and other "acting-out" behavior by adolescents featuring a strong sexual component are frequently linked to prior sexual abuse as a child. Two, in most other respects no one-to-one cor-relation is likely to exist. Let me add that our study did not include especially violent youth (e.g., murder, rape, manslaughter), so I can only offer the subjective opinion that it is likely that a high percentage of these youths were particularly brutalized in pre-adolescence.

A third aspect of the research consisted of two psychiatrists with a great deal of experience in child abuse and delinquency issues analyzing ten case histories. The principal purpose was to bring the discipline of psychiatry to bear on vexing questions regarding the abuse-delinquency relationship. Although such analysis is subjective and not empirically verifiable, it is essential that we try to make sense of the objective data that indicates some kind of important relationship exists between abuse and delinquency.

Attempting to summarize subjective analysis is difficult, but let me simply indicate that the two psychiatrists involved found the issue of causation not only beyond their capability but something of a trap for all who might consider the abuse-delinquency relationship. What can be said is that earlier child abuse is a significant contributing factor to later delinquency and is central to remediation efforts designed to reduce levels of rage and ingrained patterns of anti-social behavior.

At some point, it must be asked what does all this mean? What are the implications for social policy and the law?

For me, a central issue is the juvenile court which is responsible for "managing" delinquency cases. In short, it is not possible for the juvenile court system nationally to meet its statutory mandate of "effecting a child's rehabilitation" and "furthering the best interest of the child" when it bases dispositional decisions on poor or incomplete information, e.g., social histories or diagnostic evaluations in which the abuse/delinquency factor as well as other key factors (IQ, learning disability) have not been examined; or worse, no social history or diagnostic evaluation at all. Thus, assigning a delinquent youth with an underlying history of physical and sexual abuse to a CETA job program is simply not going to stand much chance of resulting in the desired outcome. The same is true where a delinquent is sent to a drug treatment or some other therapeutic program that has no understanding of abuse.

So, my research project is addressing the feasibility of an amendment to state juvenile or delinquency statutes whereby courts would be *required to conduct social histories in the dispositional stage, with child abuse being one of several statutorily prescribed factors that investigating personnel raise with youth who have been adjudicated delinquent.* Therapists refer to it as "asking the right questions" and it is time that juvenile court information-gathering be upgraded to reflect state-of-the-art knowledge of juveniles. One may not always or even very often elicit sensitive information in one or two interviews, yet this is no reason not to ask the questions. Furthermore, the more child abuse/neglect is openly talked about, the more victims will come forth with information about their maltreatment.

I can tell you that with the lone exception of New York, there is not a delinquency statute in the country that directly acknowledges the child abuse factor or even cross-references abuse. It's as if abused and neglected children exist in one box, CHINS another, delinquents a third. We need to understand that very often this is one-and-the-same child with child abuse being the central life experience in common.

The task is difficult because our citizenry doesn't much care for any adolescents and especially acting-out delinquents. Yet, failure to use the juvenile court system to correctly identify a primary malady of large numbers of delinquents and embark on appropriate remediation efforts (within secure or non-secure settings) costs us, I believe, billions of dollars. Research data already exists showing that upwards of 90% of our hard core criminals, especially perpetrators of violence, were abused as children. I am similarly convinced that such is the case with many of our other dysfunctional adults, those on welfare, chronically unemployed, alcoholic and/or admittees to psychiatric hospitals. And, of course, the abused are predisposed to becoming abusive parents themselves. So, these young people cost us a great deal of money where we fail to intervene effectively.

To make my own position clear, I am not suggesting that child abuse should be viewed as excusing delinquent or criminal behavior. This is why I look for probes about possible abuse to take place within the dispositional stage only after a finding of delinquency has been made. If a child needs to be incarcerated because he/she is a danger to self or others, then the child should be incarcerated. But we need to understand that, especially with abused delinquents, "punishment" can only serve to further cement ingrained patterns of anti-social behavior by children who have already been "punished" beyond any point that most of us can imagine. So, incarceration to have any positive outcome needs to be humane and it needs to feature a strong intervention capability. We also need to be prepared to make commitments to these youth for a period of years.

In closing, I would like to briefly comment on some of the objections to my proposal for a statutory amendment. A New Hampshire judge I know and respect has said to me, in effect, "don't make our probation officers, untrained in abuse issues, probe delinquents about possible abuse, and especially don't ask us to do this unless there are going to be the resources for appropriate follow-up care." This is a strong argument against what I am proposing, and I have no simple answer. His concern reflects an ultimate societal question about money and resolve. Yet, I do not believe we can afford to skirt vital information about a delinquent that is central to his/her rehabilitation. If nothing else, courts will get better at determining "what ails the patient" and avoid wholly inappropriate dispositions.

Another concern related to the above one is that an abuse probe may trigger a traumatic reaction by youth being queried. I don't want to make light of this concern but most children build up defenses over a period of years against the abuse experience and questioning about parental behavior is not apt to render the child suddenly defenseless and totally vulnerable. Today, many probation officers and other court-related personnel are aware of the frequency of incest among female runaways, in particular, and appropriately enough inquire whether any abuse has occurred in the home. It is another step to ask all delinquents about such things.

Yet another concern is the right of parents not to be adjudged abusive *in absentia*. Several research attorneys assessed this issue within the context of our research project. I have not been able as yet to study their findings, but I do know that it is their view that an amendment such as I am proposing could withstand challenges by parents.

We might content ourselves by simply having courts defer identification of abuse histories among delinquents to treatment programs that courts use as referral resources. However, under existing statutes, it is the courts who are mandated to effect a delinquent's rehabilitation. Consequently, I am not hopeful about such a loose system of responsibility unless the therapeutic agency is specifically directed by the courts to gather certain information and, in turn, statutes direct the courts to obtain this information.

The buck must stop somewhere. I say it is with juvenile courts because for most of the 20th century they have been assigned the responsibility for promoting change within delinquent youth. I know, as others do, that there is such a thing as "rehabilitation," that destructive people can and do change. And I utterly reject those who conclude the rehabilitation experiment has been a colossal failure. These people often point to research literature that indicates no type of intervention has ever been shown to make any appreciable difference on a delinquent's eventual outcome. I find this insupportable given the failure of our society in its medical and social service schools to provide good training in adolescent care; the dearth of resources for courts to call upon; and our only just now discovering that child abuse is a significant ingredient in much delinquency. In short, our nation has yet to develop a strong treatment capability for adolescent youth in difficulty, a failing that costs us dearly.

To be sure, parallel efforts need to be made to reduce the incidence of abuse in the first instance and to intervene at an earlier point, particularly within the public schools. But given that our topic at this hearing today is delinquency, I don't think that we can avoid the crucial role of the juvenile courts. And after much thought, I see no more effective way in improving the courts' management of delinquency cases than to improve the quality of information that serves as the bases for dispositions. This means mandatory case histories for adjudicated delinquents and statutorily prescribed criteria for the content of the histories, including child abuse.

I realize that statutory changes such as I am proposing are not within the jurisdiction of the federal government. However, over the past ten years the government under its spending power has stimulated important changes per-taining to juveniles in many states. Perhaps it is time for federal legislation to condition some new or existing juvenile monies to the states on state use of social histories in dispositions. Another option is to stimulate training of court personnel in child abuse and neglect issues within the delinquency context.

In conclusion, abuse and neglect is a parenting behavior that society has singled out in recent years as being of special concern to all of us. Thus far, our concern has largely been protecting small children when the abuse is occurring. But I believe all of our child protection laws inherently embody a grave concern about long-term effects of abuse. Therefore, when some of these children get older and show up in delinquency proceedings, I think that we have to admit that theirs is a special human condition and that we do a disservice to these youth and our communities if we focus solely on their delinquency or skirt their abused condition.

Thank you.

Appendix C
Recommendations of Wingspread Conference on "Child Abuse: Prelude to Delinquency?"[a]

Research

Further research on the Linkages between Child Abuse and Juvenile Delinquency.

1. Research considering the linkage between identified delinquents and a prior history of abuse and neglect.
2. Study of linkage between being identified as a victim of abuse or neglect and subsequent delinquency.
3. Research linking specific types of abuse and neglect to specific types of subsequent delinquent behavior.
4. Research linking the victim's abuse and neglect experience (age of onset, severity, and chronicity) with his or her subsequent involvement in specific delinquent behavior.
5. Research to discover what the protectors and buffers are that enable individuals to avoid becoming delinquent when they have been abused or that help families avoid maltreatment even when the predisposers are present.

Research on Intervention Strategies

1. The effects of nonintervention versus intervention in child abuse and delinquency.
2. Research on the effects child abuse prevention programs have on delinquency rates.
3. High-risk indicators—what they are and how various settings, such as schools, can use them to select families for preventive services.

---

[a]Racine, Wisconsin, 1984.

4. Research of therapeutic interventions with identified delinquents who have histories of abuse or neglect.

5. Research of differential intervention with identified abuse and neglect victims.

6. Research on intervention with families rather than individuals in identified cases of abuse, neglect, and juvenile delinquency.

7. Research on "coercive" versus "voluntary" intervention.

8. Study of the effects of long-term versus short-term intervention.

Research on System Responses

1. Research on coordinated approaches to identification of abuse and neglect

2. Research on the effects of system responses to abuse and neglect.

3. Research on the "coercive system" versus "therapeutic system," stepping back from specific interventions and looking at the juvenile justice and protective services systems *in toto.*

4. Research on the effectiveness of public awareness efforts.

Policy

Interdisciplinary Cooperation

There must be continuing interchange among agencies and professionals in the justice system, the child abuse and neglect system, the schools, hospitals, and mental health facilities. At present many sectors are dealing with a small piece of the same problem at different points in time or from varying vantage points.

Specific and Probing Social History-Taking at Intake for Delinquency

Although family social histories are routinely required in juvenile court delinquency hearings, if the hearings are not conducted correctly, they will not yield information about maltreatment that will help determine the correct intervention. Police and probation officers should be trained to ask a series of specific medical and nonmedical questions that lead into the issue of abuse and form a picture of what type of maltreatment the child has sustained, if any.

Educational Strategies Aimed at Implementing Change
within Certain Systems to Recognize the Youth as a
Victim in Addition to Being a Perpetrator

The adolescent who has been severely mistreated and is acting out in anti-social ways can often be best understood and helped when treatment specialists know what factors in his past and present his delinquent acts are a reaction to. This does not mean the abused delinquent is a victim *instead* of a perpetrator. Communicating and acting on the basis of this latter formulation would serve neither public protection goals nor the specific clinical goals for the adolescent. Health systems, school systems, child welfare systems and, of course, juvenile justice systems would be the sites for such re-education efforts.

Therapeutic Intervention for All Abused Children Who
Come to the Attention of Court Exhibiting Problem
Behavior, Regardless of the Disposition of the Case

The present drift toward stricter delinquency statutes in some states, in which community protection is foremost and the best interest of the child standard is secondary, is based on an erroneous assumption. Protection of the community and rehabilitation of the child are not conflicting goals.

Specific and Different Treatment within the Correctional
System of the Young Person Who Was Abused

In view of research documenting a high rate of abuse among delinquents, we can conclude that much of our nation's delinquent population is in debilitated condition—physically (neurologically), developmentally, and psychologically. Their problems are highly complex, of a specific nature, and require both an expanded level of awareness of the mental health and social science disciplines on the part of juvenile court justice practitioners, and trained therapists who understand abuse dynamics and the abuse treatment process.

Mobilization of Citizens to Help Prevent Child Abuse and
Child Victimization

Mobilization of the public to prevent child abuse would be carried out in the first instance through public awareness efforts such as the media campaign of the National Committee for Prevention of Child Abuse.

Early Intervention

The optimal point of intervention with an abused delinquent would be before the abuse occurred. The earliest treatment intervention we can offer the young abused child would be aimed at keeping him from becoming delinquent as a later reaction to the earlier abuse. The next opportunity for early intervention occurs when the young person comes to the attention of the court, before he becomes delinquent.

Attractive, Benign Broad-Based Intervention Styles and Services

Services are needed that do not identify the clients as abusive, abused, or delinquent. Efforts to strengthen families, particularly the development and provision of services that could be called parental education, are recommended. However, more specification is urged regarding which parenting concepts and skills are most helpful at different stages of family development and in different family situations and crises.

Broader Selection of Agencies and Institutions Servicing Violent, Acting-Out Children

A spectrum of service providers must be enticed to respond to these violent youth, in spite of their ability and propensity to elicit negative response from adults and authority figures. One means to this end is increasing public and professional awareness of the fact that most of these unpleasant youth are children who have been victimized themselves. More concrete incentives such as funds for demonstration programs in nontraditional institutions are needed also.

Interaction between Policymakers and Researchers

Researchers are sometimes channeled toward more scholarly endeavors and not given permission, encouragement, access, or time to deal with and participate in the policymaking process. Conversely, policymakers often must seize the appropriate moment to make an intuitively correct change, and cannot wait for conclusive research findings.

Translation and Dissemination of Research

Researchers in this area have a responsibility to make their work understand-able, to disseminate it beyond the scholarly journals, and to work toward utilization of their findings and against misinterpretation and misuse. It is suggested that researchers and policymakers be trained in communication skills so they can translate technical findings clearly and effectively to the appropriate audience.

Appendix D
Child Maltreatment and Delinquency: Making the Case for Preventive Criminal Justice

Hon. Betty Friedlander
Family Court Judge

s the American criminologist LaMar T. Empey has observed, a "brutal pessimism" is pervading our thinking about criminal offenders and what we should do about them. In a shift from previously espoused rehabilitative goals, Americans are moving steadily toward an even more punitive criminal justice model.[1] A growing sense that crime is out of control has brought Americans together in waging a war on crime that seems to be never-ending. People are fearful of violence on the streets and in their homes; they are frustrated at law enforcement's seeming inability to protect citizens; and they are enraged at the criminal offender who often seems to get away with murder within the criminal justice system.

New forms of criminal violence appear to be emerging, adding a climate of terror already found in many neighborhoods. Reports of unmotivated, random attacks and killings are increasing; destructive school vandalism is rampant; networks of drug gangs control neighborhoods; and drug dealing and gang warfare are openly carried on.

Crime statistics lend support to the public's perception that crime is pervasive and increasing in violence. Criminologists express concern over what they claim to be a comparatively steep rise in crime rates, especially violent crime, over the past four decades. Marvin Wolfgang, whose longitudinal study measures comparative crime rates between two cohorts of Philadelphia men born in 1945 and 1958, concluded that the cohort comprising youths born in 1958 "exhibited an escalation of violent criminality—a fearful phenomenon for the public and one resulting in a surplus of cases for prosecutors, judges, and other agents of the criminal justice system."[2]

Nothing seems to work. The 'get tough' and 'get even tougher' advocates point to a periodic decline in the crime rate as proof of the power of tough law enforcement and long prison sentences to deter the criminal offender. But few criminologists agree that tougher law enforcement is responsible for those reductions in the crime rate that we experience periodically. The concensus is that reported declines in the rate are attributable not to the effectiveness of the criminal justice system, but rather to demographic changes as the pool of the most prolific offenders—those youths between seventeen and twenty-five—shrinks.[3]

Recent research in criminology is showing that most of the programs implemented in the 'get tough' approach to criminal justice are ineffective or of limited use only. An exhaustive study of the effect on the crime rate of employing more police found "no evidence that more police reduce property or violent crime."[4] Diversion and deterrent programs have yet to be proven to have measurable effect on the crime rate by any convincing study.[5] Incarceration has been shown to have only very limited effect on reducing crime. Cohen points out, "A movement toward general increases in the use of incapacitation strategies is likely to exacerbate present levels of prison crowding. Analysis of existing offending patterns suggests that there are real limits on the maximum crime reduction obtainable under any incapacitation policy."[6] Selective incapacitation of chronic offenders by means of early incarceration is now thought to be the single most promising strategy in law enforcement, but our capacity to correctly identify those repeat offenders, at a time in their criminal careers when a period of incarceration might result in significant reduction in the amount of repeated criminal activity, is being strongly challenged. Gottfredson and Hirschi, in a recent attack on the basic premise of "career criminal' research—directed toward the identification of the most chronic offenders, whose early incapacitation could significantly affect the crime rate—conclude that this direction in criminology "has paid little in the way of practical dividends and has limited thinking about crime to the repetition of pretentious slogans."[7]

Indeed there is evidence that incarceration, rather than reducing recidivism, itself contributes to increased criminal activity. As one researcher commenting on Wolfgang's study concludes, "Regrettably, available data suggests that a high proportion of those who receive criminal sanctions continue to violate the law, committing more serious crimes with greater rapidity, than do those who were treated more leniently."[8] Nevertheless, the public calls for more and more severe penal sanctions. As one criminologist remarks, "We are using imprisonment with a . . . singlemindedness bordering on ferocity previously unknown in the western world."[9]

Moreover, despite the staggering cost of the criminal justice system (it has been estimated that the 1989 federal budget alone for the administration of justice will be $9 billion, up $9 hundred million over 1988),[10] the chances that a single offender will escape punishment have been described as "astronomical."[11] Wilson has estimated that ninety-seven out of a hundred offenders will not receive a prison sentence.[12] Yet across the country, the need for prison cells continues to outpace resources.

It is becoming increasingly clear that the criminal justice system alone cannot reduce crime. Analysts have generally concluded that the most we can hope for from our present policies is that the "impulse to criminality" diminishes as the youth matures—the process criminologists refer to as *aging-out.* In the long run, if we are truly determined to bring crime and violence under control, it is clear that we will need to rethink our total reliance on existing criminal justice mechanisms and recognize their limited deterrent and preventive capacity. Instead we will need to explore and develop alternative approaches to crime prevention that have the capacity to affect youthful behavior before it becomes criminal; we will need to develop policies and programs that will reach the child at the time when the personality is still resilient—programs that create conditions that promote the child's positive socialization and prevent those deformations of the child's emotional and psychological integrity that impede such socialization.

Despite the enormity of the problem and the complex relationship between causative and mediating genetic and environmental factors resulting in antisocial behavior, in my view it is possible to construct a feasible preventive criminal justice program based on the substantial associations between maltreatment, delinquency, and violence. I believe that these associations offer a plausible explanation as to why maltreatment contributes to crime and that they also provide a theoretical base for strategies to reduce delinquency and violence by means of programs for the prevention and remediation of child maltreatment, programs aimed at reducing the child's vulnerability to antisocial influences.

Substantial evidence already exists that establishes a significant relationship between maltreatment and later criminal or violent behavior. A group of studies, longitudinal in design, supports the finding that a disproportionate number of delinquents and violent adult offenders have experienced earlier maltreatment in some form. Alfaro's leading study is based on official records of child protective agencies and courts in eight New York counties. Two samples of children were included. The first group consisted of 5,136 children who were reported to child protective agencies or the court for suspected child abuse or neglect in 1952 and 1953. The histories of these children were traced forward through court records for reports or recorded instances of juvenile delinquency or status offenses. A second group included 1,963 children who were reported to the family court or to probation as delinquent or ungovernable in 1971 and 1972. Their histories were traced back for records of prior involvement in neglect or abuse cases. Alfaro found that 50 percent of the families reported for child abuse or neglect in the first sample had at least one child who was later taken to court as delinquent or ungovernable; and that 35 percent of the boys and 44 percent of the girls reported as delinquent or ungovernable in the second sample had recorded histories of maltreatment.[13]

Another study traced the delinquency history of 5,392 Arizona children who had been referred to a state agency because of abuse. It was found that after five years 14 percent had appeared in court for delinquency or a status offense, and after ten years 32 percent had been adjudicated.[14]

In a comparison of violent delinquents with less violent peers, Lewis and her colleagues, one of the most innovative research teams in this field, studied the medical and institutional records of violent delinquents. They found that 75 percent of the violent children had been severely physically abused, compared to only 33 percent of the less violent group.[15]

In Sandberg's study of 150 delinquents in residence at Odyssey House, a review of various kinds of records found that 98 had been abused.[16]

Becker reports that 80 percent of the adult sex offenders she was treating had histories of physical abuse as children.[17] And there are numerous self-report studies, such as a 1984 survey of 224 youths conducted by the New Jersey Department of Corrections: 77 percent reported physical abuse by their parents.[18]

The linkage suggested by these studies, which are only a small sample of a much larger body of research, is supported by studies comparing the characteristics of maltreated and delinquent children. The research suggests that maltreated and delinquent youngsters share a disturbing profile portending the difficulties they will experience in overcoming those obstacles that interfere with normal child development. The profile describes a frightening constellation of debilitating physical, psychological, and neurological defects, and a variety of behavioral disturbances—most notably poor impulse control, non-compliant behavior, aggression, and violence. These characteristics are shared by both groups of children.[19]

There is also a striking correlation between the maltreated and delinquent groups of children in the manifestation of a number of educational disabilities resulting in poor academic achievement and poor school behavior.[20] School performance is further affected by the lower than average intelligence of delinquent children, as found on standard testing, and the arrested developmental processes seen in abused children.[21]

Studies also indicate that parents of maltreated children and parents of delinquent children share certain characteristics—patterns of poor parental supervision, erratic or harsh discipline, lack of expressions of emotional warmth and nurture, and their own personal histories as victims of childhood abuse.[22] Research has also found that continuous discord, and verbal and physical aggression, characterize the marital relationships of both sets of parents, leading to unstable family units and frequent changes in residence and parental figures.[23] A uniform finding is that both family groups rank low in socioeconomic status, a problem compounded by the typically larger size of these families.[24]

These disadvantaged families are distinguished by yet another common characteristic, the absence in their lives of conventional bonds and ties such as those resulting from involvement in the life of the community, its functions, and institutions. The social isolation of parents may result in the absence for their children of "those critical experiences through which one develops a balanced web of relationships each competing for the individual loyalty within a common set of rules governing behavior on fundamental moral issues."[25]

By any standards, combined studies portray both groups of children as profoundly damaged—physically, psychologically, emotionally, and neuro-logically.[26] Hirschi, in comparing the two groups, concluded: "As far as I can determine, the gross correlates of child abuse are identical to the gross cor-relates of delinquency."[27] After reading others on this issue, one cannot help but agree that maltreatment and delinquency involve the same families, the same children.

If one considers this profile of maltreated, delinquent children and their parents in light of studies of the etiology of crime and violence—as if one were placing one transparency over another to create a composite image— one finds areas of congruence that illustrate the ways in which maltreated children may become acutely and uniquely vulnerable to antisocial, criminal and violent behavior. For example, in 1969 Hirschi formulated what has become one of the most influential theories of delinquency causation. His analysis has been adopted or incorporated into the majority of important integrative delinquency theories.[28] Rather than examining the factors that motivate children to engage in delinquent behavior, Hirschi focused on those conditions that *restrain* children from such acts. In brief, Hirschi concludes that young people are deterred not so much by the threat of criminal penalties as by their attachments to traditional figures (parents, relatives, friends, teachers), their bonds with conventional society (jobs, social organizations, religious groups), and by their involvement in and preference for conven-tional pursuits (school, work, and time spent in noncriminal activities).[29] Reading in a broad way the implications of Hirschi's theory of delinquency causation, one can identify a special vulnerability of maltreated children to antisocial behavior, often due to the social isolation of their families which limits the child's exposure to, and inclination to become positively involved in, the social world of their communities.

Other studies identify the family as the primary formative influence, and the first place to look in the chain of interacting factors leading to delin-quency. In his review of the social science literature on the relationship be-tween family life and delinquent, aggressive, and criminal behavior, Loeber concludes that "Socialization variables, such as lack of parental supervision, parental rejection, and parent/child involvement are among the most power-ful predictors of juvenile conduct problems and delinquency."[30] In a related context, harsh, excessive, or inconsistent parental discipline has been corre-lated with delinquent and aggressive behavior.[31]

In connection with the families studies bearing on delinquency, Bowlby's work on the parent/child attachment from a psychiatric perspective establishes the importance of children's relationships with their parents for their emotional and psychological development, and more broadly for their positive socialization. Dr. Bowlby writes, "I believe there is already sufficient evidence, coming from diverse and independent sources, that points to the very substantial influence on personality development and mental health of the way an individual's parents . . . treat him or her. Given affectionate and responsible parents who throughout infancy, childhood, and adolescence provide a boy or girl with a secure base from which to explore the world and to which to return when in difficulty, it is more than likely that a child will grow up to be a cheerful, socially cooperative, and effective citizen."[32] Such research, taken together with the family histories of delinquents, suggests not only a correlation between maltreatment and delinquency, but also explains the role of emotionally cold, withdrawn, rejecting, or punitive parental attitudes in bringing about the maltreatment and delinquency.

Other research into factors that predispose delinquency holds that aggression is learned behavior.[33] Parallel research in child maltreatment suggests that maltreated children develop lifelong patterns of behavioral responses in homes where violence and aggression are the usual vehicles for interpersonal communication; abuse directed against the child is frequently only one kind of parental violence, a fact that research on spousal abuse clearly indicates.[34] These findings suggest that the maltreated child learns by observation and modeling to use violence as a method of coping with stressful stimuli and carries this proclivity for violent response out of the home and into the outside world. Thus, the maltreated child may more easily resort to violence on provocation and may be inclined to develop a conscious desire to inflict pain on others in response to aversive stimuli or as retaliation for the aggression experienced by him.

In identifying factors conducive to violence, another line of research has noted that children who have engaged in especially violent criminal behavior manifest an unusual degree of neurological impairment.[35] Parallel research with abused children indicates that they too exhibit neurological impairment that is associated with impulsivity, loss of control, and other behavioral disturbances.[36] One might examine these findings in light of the work of Berkowitz, an aggression researcher who has noted the emotional, expressive, and impulsive elements that frequently underlie aggressive behavior. Contrary to the "goal-oriented" cognitive theorists who argue that aggression is carried out to achieve a particular end—for example, to obtain the respect of peers or enhance self-esteem—Berkowitz claims that much aggressive behavior erupts from an involuntary response to an aggressive stimulus, such as a weapon, or as a reaction to an adverse stimulus experienced under stressful conditions. "[I]f the situation is right, if inhibitions against aggression are weak and there is a suitable target, the adversively instigated aggression can be translated into open violence."[37] From Berkowitz one might conceptualize how the array of neurological defects of maltreated children can lower their tolerance for stress, weaken their natural defense mechanisms, loosen their inhibitions, and result in an overall reduction of the child's resistance to aggression-producing stimuli.

Another line of reasoning related to neurological defects emerges from research that identifies neurological impairments as causative factors in learning disabilities and consequent poor school performance. There appears to be broad agreement that negative school experiences are reliable predictors of delinquency.[38] While there are various theories about how poor school performance contributes to delinquency, there is general support for the observation that failure in school causes a host of negative responses in the child, which act as stimuli for further antisocial behavior outside of the school.[39] Studies showing that delinquent behavior is reduced when youths leave schools where their experiences have been negative lend circumstantial support to this hypothesis.[40]

A final link provides a theoretical explanation of how severe abuse or neglect, especially that which occurs early in life, contributes to, or may be the primary cause of, seemingly unmotivated and cruel violence that characterizes the criminal behavior of some offenders. Research with maltreated children indicates that under the stress of chronic maltreatment, the child may adopt a variety of psychological defenses to insulate himself from the physical and psychological pain of the experience.[41] For example, the child may identify with the abusing parent or rationalize the abuse by blaming himself and transforming the abuse into deserved punishment. Of all defenses for maltreatment, perhaps the most damaging is dissociation. Dissociation can be defined as a defense mechanism for coping with stress, "whereby the thoughts, feelings, and experiences are not integrated into the individual's awareness or memory in a normal way."[42] In the context of abuse, it has been hypothesized by Braun that a "traumatic event such as child abuse, may stimulate a state of overwhelming anxiety, to which the individual with dissociative capacity may respond defensively by dissipating aspects or the entirety of his or her conscious experience of the traumatic event."[43]

Dissociation may result in a variety of psychological and behavioral manifestations that range from amnesia to multiple personality states. Early exposure to traumatic events such as severe maltreatment has been described as a necessary condition for the development of the most severe dissociative states.[44] It is possible that in the overwhelming anxiety experienced by the abused child, and in the variety of the child's dissociative responses to that anxiety, we may find explanations for the cruelty of the violent offender and the link from abused to abuser.

What use can be made of these perspectives on maltreatment, delinquency, and violence in constructing a preventive approach to criminal justice? First and foremost they show that the influences that have the most profound impact on the child's opportunities for positive socialization are those experienced earliest—the parent-child relationship and the family's emotional climate. Indeed, it has been argued that the earliest parent-child attachment and interactions may have a more powerful effect on emotional and psychological development than traits that are inherited. Bowlby says, "The evidence points unmistakeably to the conclusion that a host of personal characteristics traditionally described as temperamental and often ascribed to heredity are environmentally induced. . . . The evidence is crystal clear from repeated studies that infants described as difficult during their early days are enabled by sensitive mothering to become happy easy toddlers. Contrariwise, placid newborns can be turned into anxious, moody, demanding, or awkward toddlers by insensitive or rejecting mothering. . . . Those who attribute so much to inborn temperament will have to think again."[45]

The overriding importance of the quality of the early parent-child relationship and its enduring effect on the child is supported by current research in the disciplines of biology and psychiatry. In a recent essay on the relationship between psychiatry and neuroscience, Pardes points out that "Behavioral events such as sensory stimulation, deprivation, and learning have profound biological consequences causing an effective disruption of synaptic connections under some circumstances and a reactivation of connections under others."[46] This lends added significance to Bowlby's observation that, unless a poor parent-child attachment is moderated early in the mother-child relationship by outside influences, "both the inadequate pattern of attachment and the personality features that go with it become increasingly a property of the child himself or herself and increasingly resistant to change."[47]

I would argue, therefore, that the most important change in our current crime prevention theories must be to shift the emphasis from the adolescent who already displays anti-social behavior, aggressive and criminal tendencies, to the child and his environment during those early, and critical, developmental periods. We must adopt a larger perspective on crime prevention approaches by taking into account powerful, antecedent influences that affect a child's development through adolescence and into adulthood. Numerous studies describe the continuing psychological manifestations of abuse in children from preschool age through adolescence, including the aggression and condoning of violence often found in abused delinquents.[48] What an integrative perspective on child maltreatment and delinquency makes clear is that by focusing on the immediate and direct consequences of maltreatment, rather than adopting a long-range plan for crime prevention and remediation—a plan to include both past and future—we overlook a direct avenue to crime prevention that becomes less and less accessible as the child grows older.

Yet even if we accept this dynamic, time-oriented view of maltreatment and delinquency, even if we are convinced that the child will show the effects of maltreatment in the form of antisocial behavior in the future, even if this theoretical case for preventive criminal justice can be sustained, we must still consider what kinds of actions are *feasible*. What, in practical terms and in light of our strained economy and budget-cutting priorities, can be achieved where the task at hand is no less than to effect major changes in the attitudes and behavior of individuals whose lives are so disadvantaged?

One compelling direction for an integrative approach to maltreatment/ delinquency prevention brings together Hirschi's social-bonding theory of re-straints on criminal behavior arising out of family, community, and institutional loyalties and attachments, and themes from the school of social ecology led by Bronfenbrenner, and studies by Garbarino in the field of maltreatment. These ecologists have been urging a shift in the emphasis of maltreatment programs, from relying solely on instruction, direction, and sanctions to modify parents' behavior, to changing the parents' social and human environment, and thus to changing indirectly their attitudes and ca-pacities for rearing and nurturing their children.[49]

The design of Old's highly successful multifaceted program for disadvan-taged new mothers is based on social ecological principles. Specially trained nurses visit the mother in her home twice a week where they instruct her in child development and monitor the child's progress. They also assist the mother in expanding her social relationships by helping her to establish net-works among family and friends and in the community, and they direct her to avenues for educational and vocational improvement. The program has been enormously successful. When compared with the control group, there was an overall improvement in the child's temperament and cognitive devel-opment; there was less frequent need for emergency room treatment; and the mother's sense of self-reliance and competence was increased. Educational and vocational opportunities for the mother were also improved resulting in a reduction in the mother's dependence on welfare, and a reduction in the number of unwanted pregnancies. Despite the pervasive influence of a com-munity environment where high rates of unemployment, drug abuse, and other antisocial conditions are rampant, this integrative approach to the mother's entire life situation was able to change critically the course of events her life would normally follow and to break a pattern of behavior in which she had been previously trapped.[50]

There are other programs that focus indirectly on the social environment rather than directly on the parent. Cochran's Family Empowerment Project successfully utilizes visiting social workers to help urban families with young children to locate community resources.[51] "Family life" community programs have been able to apply a social approach to teaching child-rearing skills to parents by bringing them to a place away from the home for parent education and life skills courses. In this enriched environment, in the companionship of others, abusive parents, or parents at risk for maltreatment, may attend a daycare center with their child and receive the guidance and support of trained counselors. Such programs provide parents with opportunities to socialize with other parents who may have similar stresses and learn in a supportive setting positive approaches to discipline, the importance of nurturing their children, and practical skills that may be useful in the home. In addition, their need for vocational, medical, and psychological services may be identified and appropriate referrals made.

This concept of empowerment can also be directed at young children, to reinforce positive habits of social interaction and academic excellence. The Ypsilanti Early Education Program is an outstanding example of early education, or "head start," programs that introduce disadvantaged children and their families to a world of new achievements and relationships through a highly motivated teaching staff. A recent report by Schweikart demonstrates that a well-designed curriculum for preschool children may not only enhance their positive social skills but improve their intelligence scores. Schweikart found in programs where children participated in planning daily activities, an increase of 27 percent on standard intelligence tests was achieved.[52] This finding, even though the scores decreased somewhat over time, has a special significance in light of those studies that show the impact of poor academic achievement on the child's potential for delinquency.

Multifaceted programs using strategies of parent and child social and personal empowerment have the potential, it has been shown, to affect both abuse and delinquency rates. In his nurse home-visitation study, Olds reports that the abuse rate in the control group was 19 percent, while the abuse rate was only 4 percent in the group of mothers surrounded by a network of helping relationships and contacts.[53] The Ypsilanti Perry School project, which dealt with disadvantaged three-year-olds, reports in a survey of these children at the age of nineteen, that the arrest rate of the group that had received special education was 20 percent less than that of the control group.[54]

I would maintain that the studies on learned aggression suggest similar possibilities. We are already trying to identify and assess program measures that affect the cycle of intrafamily violence. But here, too, an expanded concept of education, combined with vocational and other services, could help parents trapped in a tradition of family violence to improve their personal communication skills and vocational opportunities in order to reduce the stresses that trigger the intrafamily violence.[55] Similarly, a life-skill approach to parenting could be taught school children in order to prepare them for the stresses of parenting, to teach them how to nurture and discipline children, and to improve their social and vocational opportunities.[56]

Finally, we must consider how to implement the findings that both maltreated and delinquent children carry a disabling burden of physical, neurological, and psychological impairments, particularly the findings that children with these deficiencies are both failures in school and prone to overreacting with aggressive and violent behavior. Although we have research that documents the prevalence of neurological and psychological impairment in delinquent and particularly violent children, Lewis's study shows that these conditions often go undiagnosed *despite* records of previous medical and psychiatric attention.[57] Her studies underscore the importance of full medical, neurological, and psychiatric evaluation and treatment for maltreated children and delinquents. We must ask ourselves whether the necessary effort has been made to develop diagnostic criteria for widespread use by local medical practitioners, teachers, social workers, and probation officers, in order that they may recognize neurological and psychiatric problems in the children with whom they interact. We must also question whether we have a long-term approach to the medical and psychiatric needs of maltreated children, and particularly maltreated delinquents, which takes into account the delayed effects of childhood maltreatment in patterns of maladaptive antisocial behavior in adolescence and adulthood. In our treatment of violent delinquents, do we also have an adequate protocol to uncover histories of maltreatment and its neurological consequences, which lie at the heart of the offender's continued aggression and violence?

The cost to society of our naive faith in 'tough law enforcement' to deter and prevent crime has been incalculable. The difficulty of measuring the costs of palpable consequences of crime and violence—in terms of loss of life or injury, destruction of property, increasing fearfulness and consequent decline in the quality of community life—is only part of the problem. The young lives wasted in crime and violence are the greater tragedy, the social and moral costs of which are impossible to determine. Yet as Empey notes, a frightened public seems disinclined to look beyond the discredited mechanisms of law enforcement "to make greater use of traditional moral nets like home and school and to take a greater interest in nurturing, committing and supervising young people."

But there may be stronger public support for an interventionist crime prevention program based on preventing maltreatment. There is now a broad consensus in this country that child maltreatment should be eradicated as a matter of altruistic concern for children. A focus on maltreated children eliminates doubts about the proper targeting of efforts and fundings, for the pool of children and families is already well defined in law, research, and social work practice. Moreover, maltreatment prevention and child care programs already exist with established sources of funding and support, both nationally and in the community.

In short, the existing child protective system provides both accepted theoretical bases and established practical mechanisms for alternative crime prevention strategies based on early intervention to disrupt the interrelated cycles of maltreatment and delinquency. What is lacking in tapping the crime-prevention potential of the child protective system, however, is a public agenda, a public impetus, which can only be derived from a broad public understanding of the ways in which the prevention and treatment of child abuse and neglect go beyond the protection of the individual child, and reach to the core of community safety, security, and stability.

How can the public be informed? How do we overcome the public's reluctance to consider alternative crime prevention strategies? I believe we need, first and foremost, to develop an enlarged, interdisciplinary working environment in which the resources of the fields of child development, social work, criminology, and medicine could be brought together to generate funding, promote research, and give direction for integrative programs and policies in child maltreatment and delinquency prevention.

A professional joining of forces could demonstrate effectively that distrust of early intervention approaches to crime prevention is misplaced. The enlarged professional community can make clear, from a wide variety of perspectives, how little proof we have that traditional law enforcement mechanisms are effective deterrents to crime. It can disseminate information about programs that are effective in maltreatment prevention, in the reduction of the correlates of maltreatment and delinquency, and in the reduction of delinquency rates. In short, it can highlight for public information, the contrast between the limited proof that mechanistic application of a "get tough" approach can deter or prevent crime, and the concrete theoretic and practical underpinnings for the promise of crime prevention based on family-oriented intervention strategies.

The foundation for a maltreatment prevention initiative has already been laid down; the institutional structures—judicial and child welfare institutions—already exist; the public will to intensify the war against maltreatment is strong. What is needed is a catalyst to persuade the public of the necessity of changing fixed views on crime control to include a broader awareness of the relevance of maltreatment prevention strategies to the socialization of children and the prevention of crime. We in the professional community must provide the catalyst.

Society requires that children, as well as adults, be held accountable for their actions. We go so far in this country as to permit executions of teenagers for murder. Although many would challenge the appropriateness of a sanction of such severity for adolescents, even for murder, it is clear that the concept of accountability, and the use of sanctions to compel adherence to social rules, are among the most basic tenets of our society. Yet if children, like adults, are to be held accountable for their crimes, it is only fair that they be brought to the point where they will have the capacity to assume and exercise responsibility for their conduct. For accountability implies responsibility, and responsibility the capacity to exercise choice. It will only be when we empower children to have the capacity to choose, by dealing tenaciously with the capacity-diminishing problems of maltreatment and other correlates of delinquency at their roots, that we will be able as a society to fairly hold them responsible for their actions.

The task of reducing maltreatment and improving the outlook for maltreated, as well as delinquent, children is one of the most difficult our society faces. But it is not impossible; it is not impractical to undertake or accomplish. From the perspective of what is possible, we have hardly begun.

Notes to Appendix D

1. Gardner, M.R., "Punitive Juvenile Justice: Some Observations on a Recent Trend," 10 *International Journal of Law and Psychiatry* (1987).

2. Wolfgang, M., Tracy, P.E., and Figlio, R.M., *Delinquency in a Birth Cohort II: A Summary,* 37 (1984).

3. Cohen, L.E., and Land, K.C., "Age Structure and Crime: Symmetry Versus Asymmetry and the Projection of Crime Rates Through the 1990s." 52 *American Sociological Review* (1987).

4. Greenberg, D., Kessler, R., and Loften, C., "The Effect of Police Employment on Crime," 21 *Criminology* (1983).

5. Klein, M.W., "Deinstitutionalization and Diversion of Juvenile Offenders: A Litany of Impediments," 1 *Crime and Justice: An Annual Review of Research* (Morris, N., and Tonry, M., eds., 1979).

Cook, P.J., "Research in Criminal Deterrence: Laying the Groundwork for the Second Decade," 2 *Crime and Justice: An Annual Review of Research* (Morris, N., and Tonry, M., eds., 1979).

6. Cohen, J., "Incapacitation as a Strategy for Crime Control: Possibilities and Pitfalls," 5 *Crime and Justice: An Annual Review of Research* (Morris, N., and Tonry, M., eds., 1983).

7. Gottfredson, M., and Hirschi, T., "The True Value of Lambda Moved Appear to Be Zero: An Essay on Career Criminals, Criminal Careers, Selective Incapacitation, Cohort Studies and Related Topics," 24 *Criminology* (May , 1986).

8. Petersilia, J., "Criminal Career Research," 3 *Crime and Justice: An Annual Review of Research* (Morris, N., and Tonry, M., eds., 1981).

9. Currie, E., "Crimes of Violence and Public Policy," *American Violence and Public Policy* (Curtis, L., ed., 1985).

10. "The United States Budget in Brief," *Office of Management and Budget, Fiscal Year 1989.*

11. Empey, LaMar T., *American Delinquency: Its Meaning and Construction* (Rev. ed. 1982).

12. Wilson, J.Q., "Thinking about Crime," *The Atlantic* (September 1983).

13. Alfaro, J., *Summary Report on the Relationship between Child Abuse and Neglect and Later Socially Deviant Behavior* (1978).

14. Bolton, F.G., Reich, J.W., and Guitierris, S.B., "Delinquency Patterns in Maltreated Children and Siblings," 2 *Victimology* (1977).

15. Lewis, D.O., "Neuropsychiatric Vulnerabilities and Violent Juvenile Delinquency," 6 *Psychiatric Clinics of North America* (December 1983).

16. Sandberg, D., *The Role of Child Abuse in Delinquency and Juvenile Court Decision-Making*, Final Report to National Center on Child Abuse and Neglect (1984).

17. Becker, J., personal communication (April 1988).

18. Geller, M., and Ford-Somma,L., *Violent Homes, Violent Children: A Study of Violence in the Families of Juvenile Delinquents* (New Jersey Dept. of Correction, 1984).

19. Lewis, D.O., Shanok, S.S., Pinclus, J.H., and Glaser,G.H., "Violent Juvenile Delinquents: Psychiatric, Neurological, Psychological, Abuse Factors," 18 *Journal American Academy Child Psychiatry* (1979).

20. Lewis, D.O., Shanok, S.S., Balla, D.A., and Bard, B., "Delinquency and Reading Disabilities," *Vulnerabilities to Delinquency* (1981).

21. Wilson, J.Q., and Herrnstein, R.J., *Crime and Human Nature* (1985).
Helfer, R.E., and Kempe, H.C., *Child Abuse and Neglect: The Family and the Community* (1976).

22. Gil, D.G., *Child Abuse and Violence* (1979).
Straus, M., Gelles, R., and Steinmetz, S., *Violence in the American Family* (1980).
Rutter, M., and Giller, H., *Juvenile Delinquency* (1984).
Loeber, R., and Stouthamer-Loeber, M., "Family Factors as Correlates and Predictors of Juvenile Conduct Problems and Delinquency," 7 *Crime and Justice: An Annual Review of Research* (Morris, N., and Tonry, M., eds., 1986).

23. Rutter, M., and Giller, H., *Juvenile Delinquency* (1984).
Strasburg, P.A., *Violent Delinquents* (1978).

24. Rutter, M., and Giller, H., *Juvenile Delinquency* (1984).
Finkelhor, D., "Risk Factors in the Sexual Victimization of Children," 4 *Child Abuse and Neglect* (1980).
Gil, D.G., *Violence against Children: Physical Abuse in the United States* (1970).

25. Garbarino, J., "Child Abuse and Juvenile Delinquency: The Development Impact of Social Isolation," *Exploring the Relationship between Child Abuse and Delinquency* (Hunner, R.J., and Walker, Y.E., eds., 1981).
Hirschi, T., *Causes of Delinquency* (1969).

26. Rutter, M., and Giller,H., *Juvenile Delinquency* (1984).
West, D.J., *The Young Offender* (1967).
Hollingsworth, D.K., "The Impact of Neuropsychological Dysfunction on Child Development," *Early Childhood Intervention and Juvenile Delinquency* (Dutile, F.N., Forest, C.H., and Webster, D.F., eds., 1982).
Egeland, B., Soroufe, L.A., and Erickson, M.E., "The Developmental Consequences of Different Patterns of Maltreatment," 7 *International Journal of Child Abuse and Neglect* (1984).

27. Hirschi, T., "Crime and the Family," *Crime and Public Policy* (Wilson, J., ed., 1983).

28. Glaser, D., "A Review of Crime-Causation Theory and Its Application," 1 *Crime and Justice: An Annual Review of Research* (Morris, N., and Tonry, M., eds., 1979).

29. Hirschi, T., *Causes of Delinquency* (1969).

30. Loeber, R., and Stouthamer-Loeber, M., "Family Factors as Correlates and Predictors of Juvenile Conduct Problems and Delinquency," 7 *Crime and Justice: An Annual Review of Research* (Morris, N., and Tonry, M., eds., 1986).

31. Steinberg, L.D., "Parents: Neglectful and Neglected," 5 *Today's Delinquent* (1986).

32. Bowlby, J., "Developmental Psychiatry Comes of Age," 145 *American Journal of Psychiatry* (January 1988).

33. Bandura, A., *Aggression* (1973).

34. Straus, M.A., "A Sociological Perspective on the Causes of Family Violence," *Violence and the Family* (Green, M., ed., 1980).
Lewis, D.O., "Conduct Disorder in Juvenile Delinquency," *Comprehensive Textbook of Psychiatry* (Kaplan, H.I., and Sadock, B.J., eds., 1985).

35. Lewis, D.O., Shanok, S .S., and Pincus, J.H., "The Neuropsychiatric Status of Violent Male Juvenile Delinquents," *Vulnerabilities to Delinquency* (Lewis, D.O., ed., 1981).

36. Martin, H.P., "The Consequences of Being Abused and Neglected: How the Child Fares," *The Battered Child*, 3rd ed. (Kempe, C.H., and Helfer, R.E., eds., 1983).

37. Berkowitz, L., "The Goals of Aggression," *The Dark Side of the Family* (Finkelhor, D., Gelles, R.J., Hotaling, G.T., and Straus, M.A., eds., 1983).

38. Gottfredson, G.D., "Schooling and Delinquency," *New Directions in the Rehabilitation of Criminal Offenders* (Martin, S.E., Sechrest, L.B., and Redner, R., eds., 1981).

39. Wilson, J.Q., and Herrnstein, R.J., *Crime and Human Nature* (1985).

40. Eliot, D.S., and Voss, H.L., *Delinquency and Dropouts* (1984).

41. Fontana, V., "Child Maltreatment and Battered Child Syndrome," *Comprehensive Textbook of Psychiatry/IV* (Kaplan, H.I., and Sadock, B.J., eds., 1985).

42. Putnam, F.W., Jr., "Dissociation as a Response to Extreme Trauma," *Childhood Antecedents of Multiple Personality* (Kluft, R.P., ed., 1985).

43. Braun, B.G., and Sachs, R.G., "The Development of Multiple Personality Disorder: Predisposing, Precipitating, and Perpetuating Factors," *Childhood Antecedents of Multiple Personality* (Kluft, R.P., ed., 1985).

44. *Id.*

45. Bowlby, J., "Developmental Psychiatry Comes of Age," 145 *American Journal of Psychiatry* (January 1988).

46. Pardes, H., "Neuroscience and Psychiatry: Marriage or Coexistence," 143 *American Journal of Psychiatry* (October 1986).

47. Bowlby, J., "Developmental Psychiatry comes of Age," 145 *American Journal of Psychiatry* (January 1988).

48. Burgess, A.W., Hartman, C.R., and McCormack, A., "Abused to Abuser: Antecedents of Socially Deviant Behaviors," 144 *American Journal of Psychiatry* (November 1987).
Bryer, J.B., Nelson, B.A., Miller, J.B., and Krol, P., "Childhood Sexual and Physical Abuse as Factors in Adults Psychiatric Illness," 144 *American Journal of Psychiatry* (November 1987).

49. Bronfenbrenner, U., *The Ecology of Human Development* (1979).

Garbarino, J., "An Ecological Approach to Child Maltreatment," *The Social Context of Child Abuse and Neglect* (1985).

50. Olds, D.L., Henderson, C.R., Jr., Tatelbaum, R., and Chamberlin, R., *Improving the Life-Course Development of Socially Disadvantaged Mothers: A Randomized Trial of Nurse Home Visitation* (Department of Pediatrics, University of Rochester, 1988).

51. Cochran, M., and Henderson, C.R., Jr., *Family Matters: Evaluation of the Parental Empowerment Program; Final Report to the National Institute of Education* (February 1985).

52. Schweinhart, L.J., Weikart, D.P., and Larner, M.B., "Consequences of Three Preschool Curriculum Models through Age 15," 1 *Early Childhood Research Quarterly* (March 1986).

53. Olds, D.L., and Henderson, C.R., Jr., "The Prevention of Maltreatment," *Child Maltreatment: Research and Theory on the Consequences of Child Abuse and Neglect* (Cicchetti, D., and Carlson, V., eds., in press).

54. Berrueta-Clement, J.R., Schweinhart, L.J., Barnett, W.S., Epstein, A.S., and Weikart, D.P., *Changed Lives: The Effects of the Perry Preschool Program on Youths through Age 19* (1984).

55. Gil, D.G., *Violence against Children: Physical Child Abuse in the United States* (1970).

56. Wilson, J. "Raising Kids," *The Atlantic* (October 1983).

57. Lewis, D.O., Shanok, S.S., Pincus, J.H., and Giammarino, M., "The Medical Assessment of Seriously Delinquent Boys: A Comparison of Pediatric, Psychiatric, Neurologic, and Hospital Record Data," 3 *Journal of Adolescent Health Care* (1982).

About the Author

David N. Sandberg is a researcher and practitioner of law, all related to children's issues. His law practice includes representation of children in civil and criminal child abuse proceedings, termination of parental rights, CHINS/delinquency, guardianship, and divorce/custody cases. He is also a presiding judge in involuntary commitment proceedings.

At Boston University, where he is director of the Program on Law and Child Maltreatment, David Sandberg has served as principal investigator for two major research awards from the National Center on Child Abuse and Neglect. In addition to writing two books and numerous articles, he has presented on child abuse and delinquency issues throughout the United States and Canada.

Prior to becoming an attorney, Mr. Sandberg was involved with children's issues from a mental health perspective as chairman of a state commission on children and youth, program director, and therapist.